THE SUBVERSIVE SIMONE WEIL

THE SUBVERSIVE
Simone Weil

A LIFE IN FIVE IDEAS

ROBERT ZARETSKY

The University of Chicago Press

CHICAGO AND LONDON

The University of Chicago Press, Chicago 60637
The University of Chicago Press, Ltd., London
© 2021 by Robert Zaretsky
Published 2021
Paperback edition 2023
Printed in the United States of America

32 31 30 29 28 27 26 25 24 23   1 2 3 4 5

ISBN-13: 978-0-226-54933-0 (cloth)
ISBN-13: 978-0-226-82660-8 (paper)
ISBN-13: 978-0-226-54947-7 (e-book)
DOI: https://doi.org/10.7208/chicago/9780226549477.001.0001

Library of Congress Cataloging-in-Publication Data

Names: Zaretsky, Robert, 1955– author.
Title: The subversive Simone Weil : a life in five ideas / Robert
    Zaretsky.
Description: Chicago : The University of Chicago Press, 2021. |
    Includes bibliographical references and index.
Identifiers: LCCN 2020038852 | ISBN 9780226549330 (cloth) |
    ISBN 9780226549477 (ebook)
Subjects: LCSH: Weil, Simone, 1909–1943. | Women philosophers—
    France—Biography. | Philosophy, French—20th century.
Classification: LCC B2430.W474 Z38 2021 | DDC 194—dc23
LC record available at https://lccn.loc.gov/2020038852

♾ This paper meets the requirements of ANSI/NISO Z39.48-1992
(Permanence of Paper).

To Louisa

Contents

Preface

Three months ago, I sent the final manuscript for this book to my editors at the University of Chicago Press. Under the impact of the coronavirus pandemic, the world I knew then now seems as ancient as the Greece that Simone Weil so deeply loved. So many of the habits and happenings, occupations and preoccupations I thought were fixed forever have faded or already fled.

By the time this book is in your possibly gloved hands, these very words may seem no less ancient. The world is changing at a pace that would stun even Heraclitus. Insisting that change defined our world, Heraclitus concluded that we cannot step into the same river twice. Yet the novel coronavirus has taught us a newer truth: we cannot step into the same river even once.

Like everyone else, I am trying to keep my head, and the heads of those near and dear to me, above the white water of history. Nevertheless, in our breathtakingly changing world, a world we now divide between essential and nonessential goods, I know the writings of Simone Weil will always fall in the former category. Force and freedom, affliction and attention, community and care are more than ever ideas for our age of microbiological and ideological plagues.

These ideas led to at least one key ideal for Weil. In one of her last works, *The Need for Roots*, she wrote: "There exists an obligation towards every human being for the sole reason that he or she is a human being, without any other condition requiring to be fulfilled, and even without any recognition of such obligation on the part of the individual concerned." Few claims are more crucial for both my time and your time. And time alone will tell whether we are capable of fulfilling it.

Houston

APRIL 21, 2020

Introduction

How much time do you devote each day to thinking?

SIMONE WEIL

More than three-quarters of a century ago, on August 26, 1943, the coroner at Grosvenor Sanatorium, a sprawling Victorian pile located in the town of Ashford, about sixty miles southeast of London, ended his examination of a patient who had died two days earlier. The cause of death, he wrote, was "cardiac failure due to myocardial degeneration of heart muscles due to starvation and pulmonary tuberculosis." But the clinical assessment then gives way to what appears to be an ethical judgment: "The deceased did kill and slay herself by refusing to eat whilst the balance of her mind was disturbed."[1]

The deceased was buried in a local cemetery; a flat marker laid across her grave was engraved with her name and relevant dates:

Simone Weil

3 FÉVRIER 1909 24 AOÛT 1943

Weil's grave, its location highlighted on the cemetery map, has since become one of Ashford's most visited tourist sites. By way of acknowledging the constant stream of visitors, a second marble slab explains that Weil had "joined the Provisional French government in London" and that her "writings have established her as one of the foremost modern philosophers."

One can fit only so much on a grave marker. This is especially the case with Simone Weil. It has become a ritual among Weil biographers to sum up her life with a series of contradictions. An anarchist who espoused conservative ideals, a pacifist who fought in the Spanish Civil War, a saint who refused baptism, a mystic who was a labor militant, a French Jew who was buried in the Catholic section of an English cemetery, a teacher who dismissed the importance of solving a problem, the most willful of individuals who advocated the extinction of the self: here are but a few of the paradoxes Weil embodied. It helps to see these instances less as inconsistencies in Weil's work and life—though, at times, they are precisely this—than as invitations to reflect on both one and the other. In her notebooks, she wrote that the "proper method of philosophy consists in clearly conceiving the insoluble problems in all their insolubility and then in simply contemplating them, fixedly and tirelessly, year after year, without any hope, patiently waiting."[2]

By this measure, Weil concluded, "there are few philosophers. And one can hardly even say a few."[3] Not surprisingly, Weil held an exacting view of the philosopher's mandate. It is, she declared, "exclusively an affair of action and practice."[4] This was the reason, she thought, why it was so difficult to write about philosophy—it was, she suggested, like writing a "treatise on tennis or running"—but it is also the reason why contradictions score Weil's life. They reveal the inevitable tensions in a life that placed so great a premium on aligning ideals and practice, an effort that had to fall short sooner or later. But Weil's effort to straddle these contradictions, as well as the nature of the ideals that inspired her action, demand our attention. She was, in fact, no less singular in her insistence on accepting the consequences of a given truth than she was in her insistence on matching her ideals with her acts. As her students often heard her declare, Weil could not stand compromise, whether it was with her own self or with others.[5] In turn, we cannot stand for very long in her severe company without feeling deeply discomforted. This is as it should be. To a degree rare in the modern age—or, indeed, *any* age—Simone Weil fully *inhabited* her philosophy.

To echo the fictitious coroner's report on the death of the Jesuit priest in Albert Camus's novel *The Plague*, Weil's end remains a "questionable case." For Weil, death was neither the means nor the end to philosophy. Instead, it was a possible consequence of doing philosophy—at least if we understand philosophy not as an academic discipline, but as a way of life. As the contemporary philosopher Costica Bradatan has observed, "Philosophizing is not about thinking, speaking or about writing . . . but about something else: putting your body on the line."[6]

As with Socrates and Seneca, Benedict Spinoza and Jan Patocka, Weil obliges us to recall not just the price of the philosophical life, but its purpose. Few of us, I know, can ask this of ourselves. As Stanley Cavell wrote, Weil was exceptional in her refusal to be "deflected" from the reality of life. And yet this inability to be deflected is a gift, or curse, that most of us would gladly refuse. This is how it is—perhaps even as it should be.

⁂

This book explores five core concepts in Weil's thought. While I detail several episodes in Weil's life, I do not treat chronology as consistently as the historian in me would have liked. And so, allow me to trace in the next few pages the arc of her life.

Born in Paris in 1909, five years before the outbreak of World War I, Weil was the child of Bernard and Salomea (Selma) Weil. The well-to-do parents were fiercely nonobservant Jews who prized the city's cultural and literary life. Born in Russia to a prosperous family of merchants, Salomea Reinherz— who shortened her first name to Selma—left for Belgium, then France with her parents following a rash of pogroms in 1882.

Her family bristled with poets and musicians, and Selma was herself an accomplished pianist and singer. Bernard Weil was the child of a successful business family from Strasbourg that chose French citizenship when Germany annexed Alsace at the end of the Franco-Prussian War in 1871. Though his parents were practicing Jews, Bernard gravitated to anarchism and atheism as a young man. Although he never surrendered his atheism, he did put aside his anarchist sympathies upon becoming a successful doctor. One year after the couple's marriage in 1905, their son André was born; three years later, Simone followed. Shortly after his daughter's birth, Bernard moved his family into an imposing apartment on the chic Boulevard Saint Michel, where he and Selma provided their children with love and attention, as well as the aspirations and advantages expected of the haute bourgeoisie in Belle Époque France.

As a child, Weil both channeled and challenged her parents' values. She and André participated in discussions about music and literature during family meals, where they would speak in German and English as well as French. Before she had learned to read, she would memorize poems she learned from her mother, then recite them for dinner guests. When she was five, she and her brother were reading and performing passages from Edmond Rostand's play *Cyrano de Bergerac*. Her melodramatic performance, Madame Weil reported, reduced the family to tears of laughter. The parents found other performances by their children less amusing, however. One day, for example, the siblings went door to door, begging their startled neighbors for food. The reason, they explained, was that their parents had left them to starve.[7]

Weil's rebellious streak came to the fore early and never faded. During the war, she sent her own share of sugar and chocolate to the *poilus*, the French soldiers fighting at the front.[8] A few years later, the ten-year-old Weil slipped out of her family's spacious apartment to join striking workers who, chanting *The Internationale*, were marching along the Boulevard Saint Michel below. Not surprisingly, when she learned of the pittance paid to the workers at the summer resort where she and her family were staying, Weil tried to persuade them to form a union.[9] In grade school, when a classmate denounced her as a communist, the child superbly replied, "*Pas du tout!* I am a Bolshevik."[10]

While Weil threw herself into the world of politics, her older brother was exploring the world of mathematics. André Weil soon revealed himself as a mathematical prodigy, with his sister comparing him, not unreasonably, to seventeenth-century thinker Blaise Pascal. In a letter she wrote several years later, she confessed that her brother's genius was a source of both marvel and misery for her. In comparing her prospects to André's, Weil's spirit buckled and nearly broke. "At fourteen," she confessed, "I fell into one of those fits of bottomless despair that come with adolescence, and I seriously thought of dying because of the mediocrity of my natural faculties . . . I did not mind having no visible successes, but what did grieve me was the idea of being excluded from that transcendent kingdom to which only the truly great have access and wherein truth abides. I preferred to die rather than live without that truth."[11]

This search for truth was the winch that raised Weil from this sink of despair and, though not without halts and shudders, kept her above it until her death two decades later. It held fast during her years at the prestigious Lycée Henri IV, followed by admission into the nation's most celebrated school of higher learning: the École Normale Supérieure (ENS). Weil's classmates, who were variously awed or annoyed by her Kantian severity, called her the "Categorical Imperative in skirts." The school's director, Célestin Bouglé, no doubt had harsher labels in private for Weil. Driven to distraction by this brilliant student who tried to organize protests against the military draft, and whose drab coat pockets bristled with rolled copies of the anarchist *La Révolution prolétarienne* and satirical *Le Canard enchaîné*, Bouglé dubbed her "the red virgin." Upon graduation, Weil was assigned a teaching position in Le Puy, a small city buried in the distant region of Auvergne. Bouglé perhaps had the hope he would never again hear from or about her. But Weil had the last word. Soon after the school year began, Bouglé received a postcard featuring a photo of the immense bronze statue of the Virgin Mary standing on the cliff that overlooks Le Puy. There was no need for Weil to sign the card: under the photo was the caption: "The Red Virgin of Le Puy."[12]

Weil's militant activities were as much a trial for Le Puy's school administrator as they had been for poor Bouglé. When not teaching Descartes and Kant to her *lycée* students—fifteen girls who were both surprised and seduced by their new teacher's combination of intensity and gentleness—Weil was reaching out to the local workers. In a gesture more humiliating than humane, the city council had offered a pittance to unemployed men to break stones in the local quarry. Once Weil learned about the workers' miserable lot, she joined their protest marches. Her presence among the workers, with whom she even drank a glass of wine at a café, scandalized the notables of Le Puy. One of the local papers added an anti-Semitic twist to Bouglé's *bon mot*, declaring that "Mme Weill [*sic*], the red virgin of the Tribe of Levi, bearer of the Muscovite gospels, has brainwashed these unfortunates."[13] When the city's school director called Weil in for questioning, her colleagues and students rallied in support, while Weil herself lambasted the administration for enforcing "a society of castes" and treating the workers as "untouchables."[14] The director relented, as did the city council, which finally granted the workers the pay raise they had demanded.

Though she had won the respect of her students and won the day against the city council, Weil felt constrained in the small and isolated city. At the end of the school year, she left Le Puy for a *lycée* in Auxerre, moving yet again the following year to a post in Roanne. Both cities were as small and provincial as Le Puy, lacking the intellectual and material industries boasted by Paris. Although Weil took her duties seriously, she also found that they were too narrow, too elite, too distant from the world of working men and women. "The great human error," she once insisted, "is to reason in place of finding out." The task of finding out meant stepping outside the classroom (or, for that matter, the laboratory, library, or café). While philosophy was a matter of action, it was action always attached to truth. As for truth, Weil warned her students that it must "always be a truth about *something*"—something lived, something experienced. Indeed, inspired by the ancient Greek tragedians, in particular Aeschylus and Sophocles, Weil believed truth was something pounded into one's bones. Almost as if it were the drawing of breath, she repeatedly cited the Aeschylean line *tô pathei mathos* ("knowledge comes through suffering") in her journals and letters.

Weil's quest for such knowledge led her to work on fishing trawlers, farms, and factories. Upon finishing her school term at Roanne in 1934, Weil took a leave of absence from teaching and spent the next year working at three different manufacturing plants in the Paris region. Perhaps the only thing more unusual than Weil having sought factory work is that she was able to find it not once, but three different times in fairly rapid succession. The Great Depression battered France later than most other countries, leaving it struggling to regain its footing when Britain and Germany, by 1935, were already beginning to recover. Between 1929 and 1935, unemployment quadrupled; by the time Weil had been fired from her last position, more than 2 million workers out of 12 million were unemployed and more than half of France's 350,000 women factory workers had been laid off.[15]

Inside the walls of these dim and deafening places, yoked to machines where she was condemned to repeat the same motions countless times, Weil made one of her most disturbing discoveries: *le malheur*. Best translated as "affliction," this inhuman state was both physical and psychological. Reduced to a machine-like existence by their relentless and repetitive physical labor, workers could scarcely think about resistance or rebellion. In fact, this apprenticeship in alienation forced upon Weil the realization that the factory made it nearly impossible to think at all.

But Weil was cursed by the inability to stop thinking, even in the most awful circumstances. How could it be otherwise? If she had stopped thinking, she would have stopped being Simone Weil. Always with a cigarette, always wide-eyed behind her wire-rimmed glasses, and always with the same dress she had worn the day before (and would wear again the next day), Weil reminded her students of a simple truth: "If one stops oneself from thinking of all this, one makes oneself an accomplice of what is happening. One has to do something quite different: assume one's place in this system of things and do something about it." If philosophy didn't lead to such a conclusion, it wasn't worth the paper it was written on. Perhaps as only someone who was not an academic could claim, Weil insisted that philosophy was neither theory nor discourse, but instead was practice. This is why, she noted toward the end of her life, the activity of philosophizing is "so difficult to write about." Even more difficult, she concluded (without a hint of irony), than it is to write on how to play tennis or run a race.[16]

In 1936, the imperative to "do something about it" led Weil to Spain, where civil war had just erupted in the wake of the military coup led by General Francisco Franco. Like George Orwell—a contemporary with whom, though Orwell would not have been pleased by the comparison, she shares several striking traits—Weil joined an international battalion of anarchists defending the Spanish Republic. Though utterly incapable of handling a rifle or reading a compass, she insisted—to the dismay of those ostensibly in command—on engaging the enemy. She survived a couple of sorties, but had less luck behind the front lines. A few weeks after she had arrived, she stepped into a vat of boiling cooking oil and scalded her foot. Packed off to Barcelona, Weil was unable to find proper medical care and soon ceded to her parents' plea to return to Paris for treatment. Her foot, though scarred, eventually healed; the same, however, cannot be said for her political convictions. What Weil saw of men and women in battle left a deep and enduring mark on her mind.

It would be too simple to cite Weil's experience in Spain as a turning point, but it no doubt hastened her move away from political engagement. By the last years of the decade, she began to turn toward a kind of spiritual and religious engagement. It was not, however, to the Judaism into which, if only formally, she had been born. Instead, a series of mystical experiences—from a fishing village in Portugal and a church in Tuscany to a Benedictine abbey in France—led her to Christianity. By 1940 and France's defeat and occupation by the Nazis, Weil's attraction to Roman Catholicism quickened, while her ambivalence over its institutions deepened. This became clear once she and her parents, part of the exodus of French civilians (and, tellingly, French soldiers), reached Marseille. While the Weils began the long application process for US visas, their daughter began an equally long series of conversations with Joseph-Marie Perrin, a humane and thoughtful priest attached to the local Dominican convent. Though Perrin failed to convert Weil to Catholicism—in effect, she refused to belong to any club, or church, that would accept her as a member—he did succeed in becoming the recipient of a series of remarkable letters from Weil, published shortly after the war under the title *Waiting for God*.

While in Marseille Weil also met Gustave Thibon. Like Perrin, Thibon was a Catholic; unlike Perrin, Thibon was a farmer, not a cleric. It was Perrin, when pressed by Weil to find her a place as a farm worker, who had contacted his friend Thibon to see if he would take her on. Thibon agreed, but not lightly: he was a follower not just of Maréchal Pétain and his regime, but also the extreme right-wing movement Action Française, founded by the virulently anti-Semitic intellectual Charles Maurras. (Thibon's hostility toward Judaism, while less ideological than religious, undoubtedly influenced his decision to include Weil's anti-Semitic remarks in his edited collection of her thoughts, *Gravity and Grace*, published after the war.) Despite a difficult beginning—Weil refused to sleep in the same house as the Thibons, instead sleeping on straw in a ruined cabin on the property—and though at loggerheads over secular and religious issues, Thibon and Weil developed a deep respect for one another during the few months she spent at the farm. In Thibon's case, the respect verged on awe, while Weil trusted him enough to leave him a dozen of her notebooks.

The notebooks, written mostly after 1940, remind us that Weil's last three years were, at least from a literary perspective, the most productive of her short life. When she was not delivering underground Resistance journals or being repeatedly questioned by the police while living in Marseille, Weil wrote under a pseudonym for the literary journal *Cahiers du sud*—a necessity since the Vichy regime prohibited Jews from all white-collar professions. Weil continued to write (once again under her own name) when she reached New York with her parents in June 1942, though the writing was mostly confined to letters in which she tried to persuade close friends, casual acquaintances, and perfect strangers to either enact her controversial "Nurses Plan"—a proposal to parachute white-uniformed nurses directly into battle, with Weil leading the first group—or help her to return to France to join the Resistance.

Neither of these wishes was fulfilled, but Weil did make it as far as London. In late 1942, the Free French, the London-based Resistance organization created by Charles de Gaulle in 1940, brought her over from New York to analyze the reports sent by the several internal Resistance movements on their visions for a liberated and republican France. During the few months that she spent working at the offices on Hill Street—the better known Carlton Gardens served as headquarters for de Gaulle himself—Weil wrote furiously and surely: scratched-out words or phrases are almost entirely absent from these several hundred pages, which ranged from short proposals to the lengthy "Prélude à une déclaration des devoirs envers l'être humain"— later titled *L'Enracinement* (*The Need for Roots*).

The sheer number of proposals and papers Weil sent to her superiors overwhelmed and baffled them. For one of de Gaulle's closest aides, André Philip, Weil wrote at a level that, in Philip's view, had little application to the very real challenges that confronted the Free French. Asked by Philip to work on the vast array of problems, political and social, that would confront France upon its liberation, Weil seemed unable to keep her focus. Why couldn't she, Philip sighed to a colleague, "take on concrete issues, like those involving labor unions, instead of dealing with such generalities?" For Weil, such assignments were better left for those "who can write brilliantly about things they know nothing about."[17]

But for Weil, none of these works, despite their compelling and often unsettling insights, qualified as *doing* something about it. Writing was not enough. As Weil told her friend Maurice Schumann: "The suffering all over the world obsesses and overwhelms me to the point of annihilating my faculties and the only way I can revive them and release myself from the obsession is by getting for myself a large share of danger and hardship."[18] Her proposal to parachute corps of nurses onto battlefields was dismissed out of hand by de Gaulle, who famously exclaimed that Weil was *folle*, "a crazy woman."[19] Other efforts to persuade the Free French authorities to send her to Occupied France to work with the Resistance movements were also dead on arrival. By late spring 1943, Weil resigned from the Free French, acknowledging that she was at her wits' end.

She was also at her body's end. Her migraine headaches, which plagued her from the early 1930s, were now unrelenting, as was her refusal to eat more calories than did her fellow citizens in Occupied France, who were struggling with a spartan regimen of food rationing and a flourishing of black markets. On April 15, emaciated and exhausted, Weil was found by a friend slumped on the floor of her rented room in Portland Street. Admitted to Middlesex Hospital, she spent four months there, reading and writing with great intensity, all the while refusing not just treatment for her tuberculosis-damaged lungs, but her meals as well. In mid-August, the recalcitrant patient was transferred to the Grosvenor Sanatorium, where she died a few days later.

My aim in this book is not to offer a detailed account of this remarkable life. This has already been done by Weil's friend Simone Pétrement, as well as by a growing number of biographers.[20] Instead, my goal is to explore a small number of core themes in her thought that still resonate today. Or, I believe, should resonate. Take, for example, Weil's concept of attention. In her recently published best seller *How to Do Nothing*, Jenny Odell reflects on the so-called attention economy—a catchall term for a world now wallpapered with flat screens and steeped in mass and social media. As her subtitle promises, Odell suggests ways we might resist its overpowering allure. In one of her chapters, titled "Exercises in Attention," Odell makes the case for visiting museums. Among the artists she discusses is David Hockney, who prescribes what she calls "attentional prosthesis." In effect, Hockney urges us to think of seeing as a "positive act."[21] As an artist herself, Odell understandably looks to Hockney and other fellow artists to frame the notion of attention.

In his best selling book *Shop Class as Soulcraft*, the contemporary philosopher Matthew Crawford also dwells on the vital role of attention. His preferred site of attention is not the museum, but the mechanic's shop. "The moral significance of work that grapples with material things may lie in the simple fact that such things lie outside the self."[22] Whether the malfunctioning object is a washing machine or water heater, its virtue is found in its resistance to our fantasies of how it should behave and our frustration when it refuses to obey. The repair of a motorcycle engine and an authentic relation to the world are one and the same.

While Odell and Crawford both make eloquent cases for attending to the world—so vital an argument in a world so deeply afflicted with attention deficit disorder—neither makes mention of Weil. This is no more a shortcoming than making the case for skepticism but omitting all mention, say, of David Hume. Yet just as a new book on skepticism risks reinventing the arguments made by Hume—and doing so less compellingly—so too with a book on attention that ignores Weil. Few thinkers have attended to the subject of attention as long and lucidly as this French thinker, and even fewer have made a more persuasive and paradoxical case for doing nothing as the most effective means for doing something lasting and important.

Very much the same can be said for a number of other ideas to which, over the course of her all too short life, Weil paid much attention. My plan is to attend to a handful of these, as well. Each of the following five chapters is devoted to an idea that Weil explored in her writings and often experienced in her life:

affliction, attention, rootedness, resistance and goodness. Inevitably, the terms often spill into one another. It is impossible, for example, to discuss the act of resistance without touching on either the means for such an act—which involves attention—or its end, which implies the good. Similarly, affliction is often the consequence of rootlessness. Moreover, while Weil clearly made most of these concepts her own, this is not the case with resistance. Though she spent the last years of her life in increasingly desperate efforts to join the Resistance, Weil wrote little on the topic of resistance. The word crops up only rarely in her writings, but I find that it is a value that girds a great deal of her thought and merits a chapter of its own.

The reader, I hope, will thus forgive the occasional instances of blurred borders or crossed concepts. I also hope the reader will find that I have managed to convey these ideas in a manner that does some justice to the remarkable mind that first expressed them. Few thinkers, I believe, have managed Weil's trick of being so convincing yet subversive, eloquent but abrasive, and impractical yet persuasive. More than half a century ago, the novelist and philosopher Iris Murdoch declared that to read Weil "is to be reminded of a standard."[23] My goal is to show why this remains even more the case today.

CHAPTER ONE

The Force of Affliction

Howl, howl, howl, howl.

SHAKESPEARE'S KING LEAR

*Thought flies from affliction as promptly
and irresistibly as an animal flees from death.*

SIMONE WEIL

In December 1934, Auguste Detoeuf interviewed an applicant for a job at one of his factories. Ordinarily, Detoeuf did not make hiring decisions—he was, after all, the director of Alsthom, France's largest maker of electric equipment. Yet little was ordinary about Detoeuf. A graduate of France's elite engineering school, the École Polytechnique, Detoeuf neither talked the talk nor walked the walk of French industrialists. He dressed, as one friend sighed, like a Romantic violin virtuoso, and considered himself an intellectual *manqué*.[1]

Detoeuf no more belonged behind this particular desk than the job applicant belonged in front of it. It was not because the applicant was a young woman—legions of women, after all, labored in French factories. Instead, it was because the young woman was a graduate of France's other elite school, the École Normale Supérieure—which, like the Polytechnique, had been founded by Napoleon—and that she had, until recently, worked as a philosophy professor. Yet, the applicant was hell-bent on finding factory work, with or without Detoeuf's help. Given the applicant's bad eyesight, crippling migraines, and poor manual dexterity, he decided it was better if he helped.

On the frigid morning of December 4, 1934, Simone Weil thus began work at the Alsthom factory on the Rue Lecourbe, the clanking of her stamping press adding to the din of this industrial neighborhood in southwestern Paris. That night, on the first page of her "factory journal," Weil inscribed two epigraphs. The first is hers: "Not only should man know what he is making, but, if possible, he should see how it is used—see how nature is changed by him. Every man's work should be an *object of contemplation* for him." The second, in Greek, is Homer's: "Much against your will, under pressure of harsh necessity."[2]

⁙

The students Weil had taught the previous year in Roanne, a small industrial city in southeastern France, would not have been surprised by their teacher's change of profession. Holding her class outdoors, in a garden pavilion adjacent to the school, Weil had led her half-dozen students—who had playfully inscribed "No one admitted unless he knows geometry" over the lodge's door—in exploring geometry as well as philosophy problems. Their conversations, recalled one of her students, Anne Reynaud, were frequently interrupted by the headmistress, "looking for grades that Simone Weil usually refused to give." Reynaud, who published her notes from her class with Weil, remembered the "family atmosphere" of these classes and the deep attachment she and her fellow students felt for Weil. The method of teaching, according to Reynaud, always reflected "an inner discipline, a search for truth."[3]

But Weil's search for truth was not limited to teaching in the confines of the school, or even the adjoining park. She also made weekly trips to the nearby industrial city of Saint Étienne, where she gave evening courses in French literature at a workers' co-op. Far from being a means of social refinement, Weil believed, the teaching of literature should be a tool for revolution. By mastering language, the worker would learn how to master his place in the world. Rather than dismissing culture as a bourgeois luxury, the labor unions should embrace it as a universal necessity. Workers must prepare to take possession of our culture, Weil declared, "just as they must prepare themselves to take possession of our entire heritage. This act of possession is the Revolution itself."[4]

Yet while Weil believed that revolution was possible, it must not repeat the "criminal mistakes" of the Russian Revolution, which she believed ineluctably led to the horrors of Stalin's regime. The workers must take ownership not just of the means of production, but also of the means of self-liberation. While Weil admired Marx's analysis of capitalism, she dismissed it as "mythological"—a millenarian eschatology that claimed that, as surely as day follows night, a classless paradise will follow the capitalist hell.[5] Hence her attraction for anarcho-syndicalism, an ideological movement that urged direct action by workers as the means to achieve power, and direct democracy of worker co-operatives as its end. She became a regular contributor to the movement's most important journal, *La Révolution prolétarienne*, and in a gesture as touching as it is perplexing, pleaded with her parents to support the struggling enterprise: "Let me point out," she wrote to them, "that in case you don't know what to do with your money, that *La Révolution prolétarienne* is flat broke."[6]

By 1934, however, Weil had come to doubt the desirability, and even the possibility, of revolution. Having thrown herself body and soul into revolutionary politics, she reemerged disabused and despairing. The savage battles between the communists and socialists, and multiplying fissures in the labor movement, helped convince Weil that revolution was a mirage. In her stunning essay "Reflections on the Causes of Liberty and Social Oppression," which she wrote that same year, Weil compared those fighting for revolution to the Trojans and Greeks fighting over Helen, even though Helen had left Troy years before, leaving behind only her shade.[7] Just as the Homeric warriors went to war over the wisp of Helen, French workers took to the streets over the ghost of revolution. "The word 'revolution,'" Weil drily observes, "is a word for which you kill, for which you die, for which you send the laboring masses to their death, but which does not possess any content."[8]

But the problem went beyond the confusion and conflicts on the left that drained the notion of revolution of any substance. It was also that a revolution, as the word literally implies, invariably comes full circle, ending where it began. Though language and law, titles and traditions might change, oppression remains constant. It cannot be otherwise, Weil observes, since oppression is not limited to a particular division of labor or social classes, but flows from *la puissance*, "power," a force as omnipresent and overpowering as gravity. Power, Weil believed, is a fundamental datum of human existence. Whether it is exercised, as it was in humankind's early stages, by nature, or by human beings as has increasingly been the case ever since, it sooner or later undoes all who come into contact with it. In her dark gloss on human nature, Weil notes that the "preservation of power is a vital necessity for the powerful, since it is their power which provides their sustenance."[9]

But here's the rub: those who hold power are never secure; faced by rivals seeking to take it and the oppressed seeking to resist it, the powerful live in a constant state of insecurity. Here today and gone tomorrow, power is a fickle phenomenon, as elusive as it is inexorable. Ultimately, it is not power itself, but the pursuit of power, that oppresses humankind. There can be no bystanders to this infernal race, one that has no term, no limit, and no proportion.[10] For Weil, this crucial insight made the gravitational pull of factories as great as that of dark matter. Precisely because it was in such places that affliction was manufactured, she was bound to experience it.

✯

Assigned to a machine press at the Alsthom plant, Weil was always falling short of her quota and always failing to satisfy her foremen. Yet she understood that the foremen were also captives of force. One of them, an irascible man named Mouquet, was as tightly wound as a coil of steel. "Only once," Weil reported, "did I see him cheerful." Moreover, Mouquet was not alone; the managers above him were no more than "machines for taking responsibility." Even the owners were not exempt from this terrible dialectic: the moment one of them modernized his factory, the others were driven to surpass him. Reflecting on the remorseless nature of capitalism, Weil lamented the "naiveté of a man who has never suffered."[11] This naiveté deepens with the failure to understand that the worst suffering is not physical, but psychological—the kind of suffering that metastasizes into affliction, turning both oppressors and oppressed into things. Men no less than women, managers no less than workers, employers no less than employees are all subject to force. It was an equal-opportunity oppressor.

The act of thinking, Weil discovered, was the first casualty of factory work. A few days into her job, she was already reeling from fatigue. At times, the unremitting pace reduced Weil to tears. In one unexceptional entry, she wrote: "Very violent headache, finished the work while weeping almost uninterruptedly. (When I got home, interminable fit of sobbing.)"[12] Weil's distress resulted not just from the physical demands of her job, but also from the rigid production quotas it entailed. She could think only about the number of washers she had to punch by day's end. Yet "think" is a misleading verb. Thoughtlessness was no longer a shortcoming of those who are free to think, but a surcease for those enslaved to machines. Thinking was an obstacle, Weil discovered, to maintaining a necessary work pace. She resented the consequences—"I profoundly feel," she wrote, "the humiliation of this void imposed on my thought"—but submitted to them. "The effect of exhaustion makes it almost impossible for me to overcome the strongest temptation that this life entails: that of not thinking anymore, which is the one and only way of not suffering from it."[13]

But despite her constant migraines and crushing exhaustion, Weil was incapable of thoughtlessness. Observing her coworkers and managers, she could not help but think about the nature of force, reflecting on the ways the factory distilled the grim inequities of French society. Most of her fellow workers were women, some of whom had names—like Mme. Forestier, who struck Weil with her imperious demeanor—while others had epithets: there was the "Tolstoy fan," the "woman who gave me a roll," and the "mother of the burned kid."[14] Their lives often spilled into the factory, like that of the drill operator who brought her nine-year-old son to work. When Weil found the boy fending for himself in the changing room, she asked the mother if he also was coming to work. "I wish he were old enough," she replied matter-of-factly. Or there was the metal shearer, who, though suffering from salpingitis, could not get a transfer from the presses—work that "irrevocably and completely destroyed her reproductive organs."[15]

The women were subject to the whims of the "big shots"—namely, the foremen. Unable to master a fly-press designed to polish metal surfaces, Weil damaged a full quota of metal components. When Mouquet ordered her to redo all the pieces, he told her to adopt a position that forced her to constantly duck her head to avoid being struck by the machine's heavy counter-weight. By the time she emptied her box of components, Weil herself felt emptied. "I had the idiotic feeling that it wasn't worth the effort to pay attention to protecting myself."[16] Shocked by Mouquet's order, Weil's coworkers signaled their "pity and mute indignation" at what had been done to her. Another time, when working at a furnace where "the flames come up to lick your hands and arms," Weil repeatedly burned herself. One fellow worker showed her how to lower the damper, while another threw her a "sympathetic smile" when the damper got the better of her. Thinking back to these simple gestures, she wrote in her journal: "What gratitude you feel at such moments!"[17]

More often, though, the working conditions bred distrust and despair. "In this kind of life," Weil realized, "those who suffer aren't able to complain. Others would misunderstand them, perhaps laughed at by those who are not suffering, thought of as tiresome by those who, suffering themselves, have quite enough suffering of their own. Everywhere the same callousness, with few exceptions." A worker's complaint to a foreman was an invitation for further degradation. "It's humiliating, since she has no rights at all and is at the mercy of the good will of the foremen, who decide according to her worth as a worker, and in large measure capriciously."[18]

These conditions, Weil grasped, bred something greater and grimmer than mere suffering. In effect, the foreman judged Weil's status not just as a worker, but also as a human being. Affliction resulted less from physical suffering than from psychological degradation. Ridden by stern foremen and driven by production goals, workers were shorn of their human dignity. Within a matter of days, Weil realized with horror that the factory "makes me forget my real reasons for spending time in the factory."[19]

Rarely at a loss for words, Weil struggled to explain her state of mind to friends. In her letters, she was reduced to describing her experience as "inhuman"; in her journal, she described the workers as "slaves." You kill yourself, she exclaimed, "with nothing at all to show for it . . . that corresponds to the effort you put out. In that situation, you really feel you are a slave, humiliated to the very depths of your being." Before she entered the factory, the Categorical Imperative in skirts might have raised her eyebrows at such a claim. Once she left the factory, a shaken woman in work clothes had come to see servitude as a near universal condition, one thrust on workers and employers alike.

⁂

Weil was not alone among her contemporaries in describing manual laborers as modern slaves. A year before Weil started work at Alsthom, another tubercular, middle-class teacher with tobacco-stained fingers published his account of life among the working poor of Paris. In 1933, the left-wing English publisher Victor Gollancz issued George Orwell's first book, *Down and Out in Paris and London*. Later explaining that he "knew nothing about working class conditions," the young Eric Blair, who had just adopted his soon-to-be-famous pen name, had decided to learn about them at first hand. "I wanted to submerge myself, to get right down among the oppressed; to be one of them and on their side against the tyrants."[20]

Having gone to Paris in 1929 to write, Orwell went broke. Rather than returning to England, where he could support himself as a headmaster, he instead submerged himself into the world of Parisian *plongeurs*—the "divers" who spent their days and nights washing the pots and plates at the city's restaurants. The daily demands were debilitating. Racing for the Métro at six in the morning, Orwell returned home after midnight on the last train. He spent the seventeen or so hours in between dodging piles of dirty plates on the floors, while scrubbing out

copper pans with sand and chains, fueled only by tea and ciga-
rettes. The small space he occupied for nearly all of his waking
hours thrummed with the hissing of the gas stoves, clatter of
cutlery, and curses of the cook. Filthy and fetid, the place was,
in Orwell's words, "suitable for a pigsty."[21]

Drawing upon his experience at the restaurant, Orwell
remarked on how little remarked such jobs are by most people.
"When one comes to think of it, it is strange that thousands of
people in a great modern city should spend their waking hours
swabbing dishes in hot dens underground." Even stranger, perhaps, to think that such places forbid thinking. In effect, the
restaurant kitchen was to Orwell what the Alsthom factory was
to Weil: a site of slavery. "A *plongeur* is one of the slaves of the
modern world. Not that there is any need to whine over him,
for he is better off than many manual workers, but still, he is no
freer than if he were bought and sold . . . If *plongeurs* thought at
all, they would long ago have formed a union and gone on strike
for better treatment. But they do not think, because they have
no leisure for it; their life has made slaves of them."[22]

As perhaps one should expect from an English writer, however, while Orwell lambastes the treatment of these men and
women, he does not dwell on the spiritual meaning of their slavery. Weil, in contrast, sees just one hand—that of blind and battering force—and the affliction it leaves in its wake. Like Orwell,
she insists that those who have never experienced affliction cannot hope to understand it. Unlike Orwell, she insists upon the
malignant and monumental character of this affliction. It overwhelms our comprehension, she writes; it is as impossible to
make a fellow human being understand it as it is to describe
"sounds to anyone who is deaf and dumb."[23] That we suffer in
one way or another is not unusual—after all, this is the lot of all
living things—but it is astonishing that we may also experience
affliction. "It *is* surprising," Weil allows, "that God should have

given affliction the power to seize the very souls of the innocent and to take possession of them as their sovereign lord."[24]

Forget the case of the *plongeur*, and instead consider that of
Job. Here is a man, after all, who, while perfectly innocent, is left
by God sitting by a mound of ashes, scraping off the boils erupting
across his body, stripped of everyone and everything he held dear.
When three friends find Job, they spend seven days of silence in
his company, at the end of which Job announces the essence of
affliction: "Annul the day that I was born." The desire to blot out
not just your life, but also your birth, helps convey the reality of
malheur. "Why give life to the wretched," Job demands, "and life
to the deeply embittered?"[25] For Weil, the book of Job "is a miracle because it expresses in a perfect form things which a human
mind can only think and conceive under the torment of intolerable suffering, but which are formless at the time and which
fade away and are irrecoverable when the suffering abates."[26]

Though his friends sat with Job during his weeklong silence,
they might as well have sat worlds away. Scrambling to explain
and justify Job's fate, they turn their backs on its true meaning. They can bear the sight of Job's oozing boils and devastated
fields, but they cannot bear to plumb the depth of the affliction
they represent. True affliction, Weil insists, is so overwhelming
that we flinch at the sight of it. We can look at it "only by considering it at a distance."[27] For this reason, Weil considered the
Book of Job to be "a pure marvel of truth and authenticity from
beginning to end. As regards affliction, all that departs from
this model is more or less stained with falsehood."[28]

But Weil could not have meant the *very* beginning to the *very*
end. If she had, that would include the frame-story: the first
two chapters describing Job's character and social status; followed by the wager between God and the Adversary to test Job's
faith; and the final chapter, which, with palpable relief, reports
God's rewards to the loyal Job as compensation for his suffering.

Unlike the poem it sandwiches, the frame-story goes back several centuries and seems rooted in folklore. More important, were it not for the happy ending, we might well have refused to read the poem in its entirety.

How like another literary work admired by Weil for its depiction of affliction: *King Lear*. The great Shakespearean critic, Samuel Johnson, spoke for generations of readers and audiences when he declared he was "so shocked by Cordelia's death that I know not whether I ever endured to read again the last scenes of the play." Hence his preference for Nahum Tate's revision of Shakespeare's tragedy, in which Cordelia survives and Lear thrives. This turned out to be the preference of audiences, as well: for the next century and one half, Tate's Hollywood version displaced the original text.

But Weil rightly insisted on the bleak original. She explained herself in a letter to a young Englishman named Charles Bell, whom she had met in 1937 at the Benedictine abbey of Solesmes. Having recently reread the play, she wrote, her admiration for its depiction of tragedy had deepened. "Lear is a man forsaken by heaven and earth, helpless, and broken with misery and shame. His suffering has something great in it, inasmuch as he is broken, not bended [*sic*]." Comparing Lear's grim grandeur as equal to Sophoclean heroes, Weil quoted several passages that breathed the "very essence of the tragedy." This sensibility culminated with Lear's last lines as he gazes on his daughter's lifeless body: "Why should a dog, a horse, a rat have life / And thou no breath at all?" Nothing can be more despairing than this passage, Weil concluded, and nothing can be more defining. Such bitterness "is better for the soul than triumph and power, because there is truth in it."[29]

But that is not the full truth. Oddly, Weil did not quote in full Lear's final lines. "O thou'lt come no more / Never, never, never, never, never." Turning to Edgar, the dying Lear then asks: "Pray you undo this button. Thank you, sir / Do you see this? Look on her: look, her lips / Look there, look there!" At this moment of supreme desolation, Lear is not alone. Like Job, the broken king finds three friends at his side: Edgar, Kent, and Albany. Unlike Job's friends, however, Lear's friends prove equal to the shattering task of taking the full measure of Lear's affliction, expressed in Edgar's closing lines on accepting the weight of this desolate moment: "Speak what we feel, not what we ought to say / The oldest hath borne most; we that are young / Shall never see so much, nor live so long."

While Edgar's truth is nearly as unbearable as it is unspeakable, in the end he has no choice but to bear and speak it. His act of witnessing is the burden that Weil seeks to assume. In her letter, she pivots from Lear's own affliction to the affliction of countless others: "Do you realize there are millions and millions of people on earth who suffer nearly always, from birth to death? It is a pity they have not learned expression; they would say the truth about suffering."[30] She did not add that this was a truth that her experience as a factory worker had stamped into her very being.

⁎

On May 10, 1940, the so-called *drôle de guerre* (phony war) that since the preceding September had existed between Nazi Germany and France and Great Britain became all too real. German land and air forces plunged across the frontiers of Holland and Belgium, routing the two countries' armies and driving their populations southward. Yet France offered scant haven: once the Panzer divisions under General Hans Guderian stunned the French military command by breaking through the heavily wooded Ardennes on May 13, France's fate was sealed. Little more than a month after Guderian's breakthrough, a hastily recomposed French government—headed by the World

War I hero, the octogenarian Marshal Philippe Pétain—sued for peace. By the time the German and French representatives signed an armistice on June 22, a vast swell of French citizens had joined the wave of fleeing Belgians and Dutch. Slowly winding their way southward, as many as 10 million men, women, and children, suddenly stripped of the laws and institutions they had always taken for granted, filled the nation's roads, the target of strafing Stukas and prey to wild rumors.

Though Paris was declared an open city on June 10, there were few Parisians left to celebrate the news. From its prewar population of nearly 3 million, Paris had shrunk to 700,000 residents.[31] By June 13, declared a police report, Paris was "almost a desert."[32] Yet it was a desert that Weil and her parents had not yet quit. Convinced that there would be another "miracle of the Marne" (a reference to 1914, when a last-gasp effort by the French army had repelled the German advance on Paris), Weil insisted they remain in Paris. By June 13, however, she realized that another miracle was not in the offing. Hurrying to the Gare de Lyon, already besieged by a panicked crowd, the Weils nevertheless managed to board the last train to leave Paris. As the crowded train shuddered from the station, Weil turned to her parents: "I would prefer it if you told yourselves that you will never return to Paris."[33] Although the parents did eventually return, their daughter's stricture proved true for herself: she never again saw her native city.

When the train reached Nevers, a city 160 miles south of Paris, the Weils believed they had put a safe distance between themselves and the German army. They disembarked and, thanks to a smaller miracle in the person of Auguste Detoeuf, who happened to be in Nevers as well, found lodging at an abandoned mill. Upon waking the following morning, they found that they had not traveled far enough: German soldiers had entered the undefended city during the night. The Weils continued to Vichy, then to Marseille, joining tens of thousands of other refugees who had, in a matter of weeks, found their past certitudes blasted and future plans blurred, their world upended and lives uprooted by the seemingly inexorable force of the German military.

It was during this period that Weil wrote her best known essay, "The *Iliad*, or the Poem of Force." The philosopher René Girard suggests that for Weil, the Homeric epic was her Old Testament.[34] The essay is a rarity, as her friend and biographer Simone Pétrement notes, because it is one of the few Weil wrote that does not directly address contemporary political or social issues.[35] Its subject is Homer's epic, and its approach is partly philological: Weil had translated the poem herself, striving to remain as faithful as possible to the original ordering of words. But Weil's reading of the *Iliad* nevertheless echoes with the rumble of tank treads and the screeching of Stukas, the confusion at train stations and chaos along the roads, the proclamations of surrender and rumors of resistance. The tragedy unfolding outside the walls of ancient Troy now seems little more than a rehearsal for the tragedy unfolding outside the walls of modern Paris. Though several millennia separate the two tragedies, their subject matter is the same: the inexorability of force and what it does to human beings.

In the opening lines, Weil announces that the *Iliad*'s true hero is not a warrior—not Hector or Patroclus or even Achilles— but force itself, as constant in the movement of human events as gravity is in the movement of physical objects. It is force that "enslaves man," it is force "before which man's flesh shrinks away," and it is force that "modifies the human spirit." For readers who have not taken full measure of contemporary events, Weil effectively collapses the vast span of time between Homer's era and her own. "For those dreamers who considered that force, thanks to progress, would soon be a thing of the past, the

Iliad could appear as an historical document. For others, whose powers of recognition are more acute and who perceive force, today as yesterday, at the very center of human history, the *Iliad* is the purest and loveliest of mirrors."[36]

Inevitably, this mirror reflects the chaos and confusion of 1940. When Weil quotes Homer's words that Hector, killed by Achilles, dies far from the "hot baths" that an unaware Andromache was preparing for him at Troy, she conjures images of French civilians sleeping on the sides of bomb-pocked roads, ignorant over the fate of their sons serving in the army. Not just Hector was far from hot baths: "Nearly all of human life, then and now, takes place far from hot baths."[37] Just as Homer allows "no comforting fictions" to intervene in his transparent account of force, Weil insists the French experienced something similar between the fall of republican institutions and the rise of authoritarian institutions: during this short span of time, there was no space for comforting fictions. While they might not have been interested in war—which was certainly the case for her fellow pacifists—war was interested in them. Having watched Paris empty at the approach of the Germans, knowing that the Germans now occupied the city, Weil grasped the enormity of this event. The entire poem, she declares, "lies under the shadow of the greatest calamity the human race can experience—the destruction of a city."[38]

Of course, Paris was not physically destroyed. The spire of Notre-Dame and the Eiffel Tower still rose over the city, the Pont Neuf and Pont des Arts still spanned the Seine, the grand boulevards still connected the grand monuments, such as the Arc de Triomphe and République. But those monuments and buildings, now draped by Nazi swastikas and housing Nazi functionaries, nevertheless reflected the vast sweep of force. As surely as the collapse of the French army and confusion of the French government, these changes on the city's surface reflected the ineluctability and inhumanity of force. This phenomenon, Weil argues, "turns anybody who is subjected to it into a *thing*. Exercised to the limit, it turns man into a thing in the most literal sense: it makes a corpse out of him."[39]

Force can sweep up not just men, but even those slightly more than men, such as Achilles. Driven mad by the death of his friend Patroclus, a berserk Achilles reenters the war. Aided by the goddess Athena and armed with a newly forged shield, he rips mercilessly through the Trojan forces. When one of his victims, Lycaon, pleads for his life, Achilles replies with chilling clarity:

"Come, friend, you too must die. Why moan about it so?
Even Patroclus died, a far, far better man than you.
And look, you see how handsome and powerful I am?
The son of a great man, the mother who gave me life
a deathless godless. But even for me, I tell you,
death and the strong force of fate are waiting."[40]

When this day of permanent red ends, Achilles's thirst for vengeance does not.[41] On Patroclus's funeral pyre, Weil reminds us, the Greek hero "cuts the throats of twelve Trojan boys as naturally as we cut flowers for the grave."[42]

Yet this act will recoil endlessly across time, setting off reactions that will ruin those who began the movement. Weil tells us that Homer reveals what remains hidden to Achilles and his fellow Greek warriors: "The consequences of their deeds will at length come home to them—they too will bow their neck in their turn."[43] This is hardly a matter of justice, at least in the sentimental understanding of the term. Instead, the rule governing this phenomenon is as impersonal as the laws of thermodynamics. "Force is as pitiless to the man who possesses it, or thinks he does, as it is to its victims; the second it crushes, the first it

intoxicates. The truth is, nobody really possesses it."[44] This is
a truth that had already been pounded into Weil at Alsthom—
namely, that power runs through the entirety of human affairs,
but is controlled by no human, and that it "contains a sort of
fatality which weighs as pitilessly on those who command as on
those who obey."[45]

Ironically, perhaps, the rhetorical force of Weil's depiction
of force in human affairs obscures certain logical weaknesses.
Her situation at Alsthom, for example, was more complex than
having arrived as a human being and leaving as a thing—having
been forever branded, as she insisted, as a slave. Just as Orwell
knew while living down and out, so too with Weil: they both
could leave this world when they wished. Although Weil's fellow
workers did not enjoy this same freedom, they nevertheless had
not been rendered inert. After all, the volcanic strikes of 1936,
which brought the nation to a standstill and the Popular Front to
power, channeled the deep and abiding nature of human agency.
Moreover, the relentless demands at the factory—a force that
drove managers as mercilessly as it did workers—made it all too
easy for all parties to transgress the standards of human dignity and decency. When we witness such transgressions, Peter
Winch notes, we tend to say: "They are not behaving as human
beings." But we do not mean they have stopped *being* human
beings. Instead, our meaning is more modest, if not more
comprehensible—namely, that our fellow human beings have
fallen short of our shared measure of humanity.[46]

Weil nevertheless holds so fast to her fundamental claim that
she sometimes tweaks the letter and spirit of Homer's poem. In
her depiction of the scene between Achilles and Lycaon, we are
especially chilled by Weil's observation that the Greek hero is
pointing his spear at the vanquished Trojan. But a glance at the
poem reminds us that that same spear is, in fact, lodged in the
ground behind Lycaon, heaved just moments earlier by Achil-

les. Or, again, there is the nearly unbearable scene where Priam appears at Achilles's tent to ask for the return of the body of his slaughtered son Hector. When the Trojan king kneeled before Achilles and clasped his knees, Achilles, Weil reports, took the old man's arm and "pushed him away." It was not insensibility, she explains, that made Achilles do what he did. Instead, it was a "question of his being free in his attitudes and movements as if, clasping his knees, there were not a suppliant but an inert object." The glitch with this gloss, however, is that Weil herself pushed away a crucial word—one rescued by the classicist Robert Fagles in his translation of the poem: "Taking the old man's hand / he gently moved him back."[47]

Though Weil at times does do violence to the text, she does so to capture what happens when we do violence to one another. This is especially the case for the forms of violence that the infernal incubator of the twentieth century repeatedly hatched. With stunning prescience, she grasped the existential consequences of totalitarianism, whether enacted in Stalin's Russia or Hitler's Germany. No two nations, she warned, "are more similar in structure"; the totalitarian state "seizes control of almost every department of individual and social life; in each there is the same frenzied militarization, and the same artificial unanimity, obtained by coercion." Moreover, in both societies the true believers are "resolved to die, and above all to kill" the other side, and any other group identified as a threat.[48]

Like Orwell and Camus, Weil was an isolated voice on the left who denounced communism with the same vehemence as she did fascism. As for those apologists who insisted that Stalinism was a perversion of Marxism, Weil was merciless. "Descartes used to say that a clock out of order is not an exception to the laws governing clocks, but a different mechanism obeying its own laws. This is how we should regard Stalin's regime: not as a worker's state out of order, but as a different social mechanism. Its definition is found in the wheels that compose it and which functions according to the nature of those wheels."[49] One might as well insist that racism is a perversion of ethno-nationalism, or, for that matter, that Trumpism is a perversion of populism. In all of these cases, the line of causality is straight and sharp.

⁂

"Affliction constrains a man to ask continually 'Why'—the question to which there is essentially no reply."[50] Weil's observation uncannily anticipates the experience of the Italian writer and Auschwitz survivor Primo Levi. When he reached his hand outside his cell window at Auschwitz to break off an icicle to slake his thirst, a guard knocked it out of his hands. When Levi asked why, the guard replied: *"Hier ist kein warum* [There is no why here]."

Had she lived long enough to learn about the nature and extent of the Final Solution, Weil would not have been shocked. While the methodical deliberation and technological devices that help define Auschwitz are unique, a state's determination to exterminate entire peoples is not. History sags under the weight of premeditated acts of unspeakable inhumanity. Weil considered the Albigensian Crusade to have been one instance of such behavior. During the war, Weil wrote two essays on the civilization of medieval Languedoc, the source of a brilliant literary tradition—distilled in the songs of the troubadours—and the home of a beguiling religious sect known as the Cathars. In their break from the papacy, the Cathars practiced a rigorously purified form of Christian belief. Convinced of the danger presented by the Cathars, the Roman Church and French monarchy launched the so-called Albigensian Crusade, which succeeded in both enriching its participants and exterminating the Cathars, leaving in its murderous wake "a few troubadour songs, a few texts concerning the Cathars, and some marvelous churches."[51] Another writer, Zoe Oldenbourg, captured the nature of this crusade in her description of the burning of hundreds of Cathars at the fortress of Montségur: "In a few hours' time the two hundred living torches heaped together inside the palisade were no more than a mass of raw, blackened, bleeding flesh, slowly burning to a cindered crisp, spreading a ghastly stench of burnt meat right down the valley, and up to the very walls of the fortress."[52]

In the summer of 1942, the journal *Cahiers du sud* published Weil's essays on the Cathars under the pseudonym Emile Novis. The reason for this subterfuge was the same reason why Weil was no longer in France: she was a Jew who, largely for the sake of her parents, had fled France for the United States. And yet, in an irony become a source of bitter controversy among Weil's readers, she did not consider herself Jewish. She made this clear whenever the occasion presented itself, perhaps most notably in her letter to Jérôme Carcopino, the minister of education. Forbidden by Vichy's anti-Semitic laws to teach in the public schools, Weil patiently explained that she was not Jewish by religious or racial definition, failing to see any racial link with "the people who lived in Palestine two thousand years ago." In fact, she said that if "there is a religious tradition I consider as my patrimony, it is the Catholic tradition."[53]

Not surprisingly, Weil never received a reply. More surprising, perhaps, is that Weil had not only come to see Catholicism as part of her French patrimony, but that she had also come to make it both the substance and scaffolding of her worldview. Of course, this was not always the case. When she was still a student, Weil observed, "I saw the problem of God as a problem the data of which could not be obtained here below, and I decided that the only way of being sure not to reach a wrong solution, which seemed to me the greatest possible evil, was to leave it alone. So I left it alone."[54] But the problem, if that is the word, would not leave her alone. Shortly after she reemerged, exhausted and emptied, from her factory experience in 1935,

Weil accompanied her parents to Portugal. Finding herself in a "wretched" coastal village one evening, she watched as the wives of the fishermen performed a religious ritual, going from boat to boat while singing "ancient hymns of a heart-rending sadness." At that place and moment, Weil declared, "the conviction was suddenly borne in upon me that Christianity is preeminently the religion of slaves, that slaves cannot help belonging to it, and I among others."[55]

In short order, this desolate epiphany led to two others, most notably her experience in 1938 at the abbey of Solesmes in northern France. Battered by her migraines, she spent ten days attending all of the liturgical services, plunging herself into the chants. Even though, or perhaps because, "each sound hurt me like a blow, by an extreme effort of concentration I was able to rise above this wretched flesh, to leave it to suffer by itself, heaped up in a corner, and to find a pure and perfect joy in the unimaginable beauty of the chanting and the words." Solesmes served as an immersion course in the nature of Christian love—a course Weil left with "the thought of the Passion of Christ [having] entered into my being once and for all."[56] To Joseph-Marie Perrin, Weil confessed she had "never foreseen the possibility of . . . a real contact, person to person, here below, between a human being and God."

For many readers, this "contact" marked a rupture in Weil's thought, one that carves a frontier between her philosophical and theological approaches to the human situation. But for others, it is less a break than a broadening of the same concerns that had always driven her thought. This seems especially the case with her notion of *malheur*. For Weil, what fed the flames of the auto-da-fé at Montségur were not, or were no longer, human beings. Instead, the foreign invaders had, just as Achilles had done to the Trojans, turned what had once been human beings into things. This is how affliction works: it "deprives its victims of their personality and makes them into things."[57]

There is nothing metaphysical about this notion, which perhaps makes it all the more difficult to comprehend. Affliction, like fire, can ultimately consume our physical selves, but unlike fire, it begins by destroying our social and psychological selves. At its extreme, it reduces us, if not to a dead husk of what we once were, to something equally gruesome: a being driven by nothing more than the instinct of survival, one that "blindly fastens itself to everything which can provide it with support, like a plant fastens its tendrils." Dissatisfied with this simile, Weil reaches more deeply for one to convey the dreadfulness of this state. A human being crushed by *malheur* is "hideous as life in its nakedness always is, like an amputated stump, like the swarming of insects."[58]

As dire as this scene appears, it becomes even more so when viewed through the prism of religious faith. As long as one "leaves alone" the question of God, as Weil had done through most of her life, the presence of affliction in our lives is harrowing, but not especially puzzling. It is the unavoidable consequence of a world governed by forces largely beyond our comprehension, not to mention our control. When we add God to this mix, however, we transform a dismal but clear-cut state of affairs into a dismal but confounding state of affairs. This was, as Weil and we understand, Job's predicament.

What are we to think and do, if this play of necessity and preponderance of affliction is God's handiwork?

⁂

A consideration of the question—one that will not offer an answer, for there is not one—must wait. For now, what is puzzling is Weil's conflicted attitude toward *malheur*. On one side, there is nothing to be said on behalf of affliction. Weil insists that it is ground zero of human misery. No state is more devastating for a human being because no other state so utterly denies our very humanity and destroys our very sense of self. "Nothing in the world can rob us of the power to say 'I.' Nothing except extreme affliction."[59] It is the mark of slavery, one too hideous for those who have so far escaped this condition to gaze upon. The only reactions it arouses are "disgust, horror and scorn."[60] Or, quite simply, it scares others away from the afflicted person: "The sight of an afflicted man frightens away every kind of attention."[61] There is, Weil writes, just one observer capable of looking on the face of destitution: "It is only God who can pay attention to an afflicted man."[62]

Yet there is another and disturbing side: Weil believes that something can be said for *malheur*. She pays an unsettling amount of attention to this condition, at times too attached to both the concept and the reality it seeks to capture. Rather like Victor Frankenstein, she is both outraged and obsessed by this (in her case) conceptual creation. There is an element of morbidity lurking in her description of affliction, one that can lead, as Mary Dietz notes, to the risk of fetishizing it.[63] Someone familiar with Weil's tendency toward extremism was Auguste Detoeuf. In 1936, two years after her factory experience, Weil told her old employer about a conversation between two business owners she had overheard in a train. Complaining about the strikes then sweeping France, these two "well fed and well dressed" men believed they had everything to lose should the strikers succeed. That workers should demand their rights, Weil marveled, was nothing more than a "monstrous injustice" for these comfortable and corpulent owners.

In his reply, Detoeuf agreed that many employers lacked a sense of civic duty and social obligation. Yet, he also suggested that Weil failed to show these employers the same attention she gave to the workers. Leave aside, he urged her, "whatever may be rather grotesque and odious in the fact of being portly and well-nourished." If Weil put herself in their place, she would find that "unless these men were more than human they could hardly think and feel otherwise." Convinced their material well-being was at risk, they responded as Weil would respond if her mental well-being was threatened. They truly believed the end of their world—the *only* world, for them—was nigh. "You must really use your own imagination to try to grasp that these men have not so much imagination as you credit them with. For them, to have nothing more to lose means to have to give up everything that makes up their existence."[64]

Detoeuf had a point. The limitation to Weil's imagination is, paradoxically, its seeming limitlessness. Her ability to plumb the human condition runs so deep that it risks losing those of us who remain near the surface of things. In an unpublished text, Weil makes clear she was aware of this problem. "Our personality," she wrote, "seems to us a sort of limit . . . but it also appears to us a support, and we wish to believe there are things we would never be capable of doing or saying or thinking because it is not in our character." This, she closes laconically, "often proves false."[65] The force of necessity, as we have seen, can shatter these expectations, along with our personalities, from one day to the next.

Behind this laconic conclusion lies a raw truth. We might debate whether Weil dwelt too long and deep on affliction, but what seems less debatable is the inconvenient truth it underscores. Though it takes many shapes, *malheur* exists as assuredly as do the many strategies we employ to deny it or to distract ourselves from it. Weil insisted that in and of itself, affliction does not hold any value whatsoever. Its value, instead, lies in the use we make of it. Whether it can teach us anything as grand as wisdom depends on how we define wisdom. If virtues like comprehension and compassion, toleration and moderation are to constitute at least part of wisdom, we could do worse.

CHAPTER TWO

Paying Attention

It is a task *to come to see the world as it is.*

IRIS MURDOCH

Refuse to be an accomplice.
Don't lie—don't keep your eyes shut.

SIMONE WEIL

When she settled in Marseille in the late spring of 1941, Weil gravitated toward the world of underground activity. She began to attend the semi-clandestine meetings of the Société d'Études Philosophiques, a group of intellectuals and academics formed by the industrialist Gaston Berger. At the same time, she persuaded a friend, the poet Jean Tortel, to help her make contact with a local Resistance network. Though he doubted that Weil's abilities matched her aspirations when it came to active resistance, Tortel found her request irresistible. Several years later, he recalled that he and his colleagues had found Weil to be "rather formidable and fearsome." This was, in particular, true of her eyes: "Through her glasses, she looked at you (when she did look) . . . with an intensity and, also, a kind of inquisitive greediness that I have never experienced with others." Her gaze, Tortel confessed, "was nearly insupportable. In her presence, lies were quite simply excluded."[1]

This portrait of Weil reminds us that she saw or, more accurately, *read* the world in a way few others do. In fact, soon after she joined Berger's society, Weil drafted a short piece titled

"Essai sur la notion de lecture" ("Essay on the Concept of Reading"). Unpublished and unread during Weil's lifetime, the essay presents reading and meaning as a package deal. Weil argues that when we read the world, we necessarily do so through the prism of meaning. No less inevitably, the prism varies from one set of eyes to the next. This is why, she observes, "we can argue endlessly about the reality of the external world, since what we call the world are the meanings that we read." By way of illustration, Weil presents two women holding nearly identical letters announcing the deaths of their sons. "The first one glances at it, faints, and until the day she dies her eyes, her mouth, and her movements will never again be the same. The second one remains unmoved; her face, her posture do not change at all."[2]

We grasp the reason for these radically opposed reactions only when we learn that while the first woman can read, the second woman is illiterate. For Weil, though, this is not reason enough. What she has so far argued would not surprise a student of Friedrich Nietzsche or Richard Rorty, but Weil then pivots in a surprising direction, marveling over the sheer physicality of the first woman's reaction. "It isn't the sensation, it is the meaning that has seized the first woman by striking her mind, immediately, as a brute fact, without her participation in the matter, just the way sensations strike us. *Everything happens as if the pain were in the letter itself and jumped out from the letter to land on the face reading it.*" The actual sensations offered by the texture of the paper or the color of the ink are utterly irrelevant. Instead, it is pain itself that "is given to one's sight."[3] It is as if the impact of this meaning is objective, not subjective, and comes not from the woman's inner world, but from the physical world outside of her. It is as real, in short, as a punch to one's head from another's fist. Yet we also know that the letter's meaning, and the visceral force it carried, depends upon this particular woman. One need not be illiterate to dodge the blow of this particular meaning; one need only not be the mother of this dead son.

Reading, for Weil, extends beyond black marks on a sheet of paper, to the world itself. In her essay, Weil considers a visual mistake we have all made at one time or another: confusing something we see for something else. For example, while walking along a deserted road at night, she glimpses a man off to the side, waiting to ambush her. Struck by this "human and menacing presence that forces itself on me," she realizes only after she comes nearer that the "man" is, in fact, a tree. This sensory confusion, Weil insists, does not unfold in two stages: first seeing and then interpreting the man-like tree. Instead, it is all of a piece: "A human presence has penetrated my soul through my eyes, and now, just as suddenly, the presence of a tree."[4] What has changed, of course, is not the world, but our reading of it. Yet that mistaken reading, Weil argues, seized her as if it were external and real. The man was as real in her reading of the road as the death of the son was in the mother's reading of the letter.

The world is flush with such meanings—meanings that, in turn, fix our beliefs and acts. They sweep over us with such force, Weil writes (in English), that "my soul is no longer my own."[5] The risk of losing our souls as we read the world is especially great at times of crisis. In a society riven by political polarization, when we see someone on the other side, we do not distinguish between that person and our hatred: they are one and the same. In times of war, we see those on the other side as worthy of death; in times of peace, we see those same beings as worthy of respect or, at least, tolerance. The force of each of these readings, Weil notes, makes it "appear as the only real, only possible way to look at things; the other one seems purely imaginary."[6] We read the world not from the heights, but instead from the ground; not with Olympian disregard, but instead with all too human investment. For Weil, the effort to achieve such distance in order to read the world is as useless as reading Kant's *The Critique of Practical Reason* in order to know whether to repay a loan. Instead, we will pay back the loan because it seems "that something in the deposit cries out to be given back."[7] In short, the way in which we read the world turns on our particular location—moral, social, political, and economic—within the world. And the world, of course, is what humankind makes of it.

Weil's concept of reading, and the epistemological assumptions underlying it, wildly differs from most philosophical accounts. Whether we are Lockean or Sartrean, we assume that sensations precede values—that existence always has the step on essence—in our construction of the world, while Weil instead asserts that values and sensations are coterminous. As Peter Winch notes, "our concepts, which give the world its shape, are unintelligible except as concepts exercised by beings whose common life exhibits certain aspirations and values."[8] This interpretation—one where the epistemological is the ethical—seems to pull the rug out from under those seeking absolute rules on how to read and act in the world. Readings of the world, after all, can vary as dramatically as the languages in which they are couched. Is there, though, far from the dizzying crowd of practical readings, a single and right way to read? Is there a center, as Weil asks in her notebooks, "from which may be seen the different possible readings—and their relationship—and our own only as one among them"? By way of a rather cryptic reply, she then suggests that we "transport ourselves to that center of thought from which the other person reads values; contemplate the values destroyed by what we are going to do."[9] While Weil is uncertain, at least at this point, about the precise location of the center, her means of transportation is what she calls "attention."

⁂

"Everyone knows what attention is," William James famously declared in his *Principles of Psychology*. For those who are not "everyone," James goes on to explain that attention is the "taking possession by the mind, in clear and vivid form, of one out of what seem several simultaneously possible objects or trains of thought. Focalization, concentration, of consciousness is of its essence. It implies withdrawal from some things in order to deal effectively with others."[10]

Though she agrees with James's insistence that attention both engages the mind and entails a kind of withdrawal, Weil would have taken issue with the claim that attention requires the mind's concentration—tensing, really—on a specific issue. For Weil, this kind of mental tautness is, in fact, inimical to true attention. In Weil's role as a teacher, we catch glimpses of what she understood by attention. For example, Anne Reynaud, one of her students at Roanne in 1933, recalled that Weil would take the class outdoors and gather them under a tall cedar tree where they would together "seek problems in geometry."[11] The phrase is telling: rather than "finding the answer," the students instead looked for problems. Reflecting upon a problem, rather than resolving it, was Weil's goal. No less telling is Reynaud's recollection that Weil never dictated to the students during her lectures, just as she always refused to give them grades. These habits were bred not from indifference, but instead from a radically different conception of attention.

While waiting with her parents in Marseille for their visas to the United States, Weil presented her ideas about the teaching of attention to Joseph-Marie Perrin. In the late spring of 1941, Weil had contacted this nearly blind Dominican priest in order to discuss the possibility of converting to Catholicism. Perrin readily agreed to a meeting, which took place on June 7, 1941, at the Dominican convent in Marseille. Between then and the following May, when she left with her parents for New York, Weil met several more times with Perrin, mostly discussing the theological and dogmatic issues that, for Weil, stood in the way of her conversion. (They almost certainly never discussed their respective participation in Resistance activities. Under Perrin's guidance, the convent became a safe house for Resistance fighters and French and foreign Jews, while at the same time he oversaw the dissemination of the clandestine journal *Les Cahiers du témoignage chrétien*.) The conversations between these two friends also unfolded, in sporadic fashion, through the exchange of letters before and after Weil's departure. In the opening lines of her first letter, Weil set the tone: "I am tired of talking to you about myself, for it is a wretched subject, but I am obliged to do so by the interest you take in me as a result of your charity."[12]

Shortly before leaving Marseille, Weil sent Perrin an essay titled "Réflexions sur le bon usage des études scolaires en vue de l'amour de Dieu" ("Reflections on the Right Use of School Studies with a View to the Love of God"). By "view," Weil means attention—the one skill all schools should cultivate in their students. But we need to attend to her understanding of the term. Normally, when we pay attention to someone or something, we undertake what Weil calls a "muscular effort": our eyes lock on another's eyes, our expressions reflect the proper response, and our bodies shift in relation to the object to which we are paying attention. This kind of attention flourishes in therapists' offices, business schools, and funeral homes. It is a performative rather than reflective act, one that displays rather than truly pays attention. This sort of attention is usually accompanied by a kind of frowning application—the very same sort, as Weil notes, that leads us to a self-congratulatory "I have worked well!"[13]

For Weil, attention is a "negative effort," one that requires that we stand still rather than lean in. The object of this kind of attention could be mathematical or textual, a matter of grasping a puzzle posed by Euclid or one posed by Racine. Whether we do solve the problem, argues Weil, is secondary. The going is as important as the getting there, if not even more so. "It does not even matter much whether we succeed in finding the solution or understanding the proof, although it is important to try really hard to do so. Never in any case whatever is a genuine effort of the attention wasted."[14] Scorning practices like memorization and dictation that impose the "right answers" upon students, she acknowledges that the practices she wished to instill in students were alien to schools in her own day (and they remain alien to most schools in our own day). "Although people seem to be unaware of it today," she declares, "the development of the faculty of attention forms the real object and almost the sole interest of studies . . . All tasks that call upon the power of attention are interesting for the same reasons and to an almost equal degree."[15]

Is it really as simple, though, as saying that it is the going, and not the getting there, that counts? For Weil this could be deeply misleading. First, she gives this notion a particular twist: by embracing the going and not the getting there, we will ultimately get to somewhere more important than the original destination. Even should we fail to solve a geometry problem at the end of an hour, we will nevertheless have penetrated into what Weil calls "another more mysterious dimension."[16] This dimension is moral: it is the space where, by our act of attention, we grasp what has always been the real mystery—the lives of our fellow human beings. Weil argues that this activity has little to do with the sort of effort most of us make when we think we are paying attention. Rather than the contracting of our muscles, attention involves the canceling of our desires; by turning toward another, we turn away from our blinding and bulimic self. The suspension of our thought, Weil declares, leaves us "detached, empty, and ready to be penetrated by the object."[17] To attend means not to seek, but to wait; not to concentrate, but instead to dilate our minds. We do not gain insights, Weil claims, by going in search of them, but instead by waiting for them: "In every school exercise there is a special way of waiting upon truth, setting our hearts upon it, yet not allowing ourselves to go out in search of it . . . There is a way of waiting, when we are writing, for the right word to come of itself at the end of our pen, while we merely reject all inadequate words."[18]

This is a supremely difficult stance to grasp. As Weil notes, "the capacity to give one's attention to a sufferer is a very rare and difficult thing; it is almost a miracle; it *is* a miracle. Nearly all those who think they have this capacity do not possess it."[19] I, for one, know I do not possess it, not only because it collides with the way I think about thought, but also because it collides with the fact that I can rarely, if ever, think about anything or anyone else without also thinking about myself. To attend to a fellow human being entails far more than thinking about or even feeling for that person. Pity, like cognition, involves reaching toward another by acknowledging her suffering. In this respect, my faculty of sympathy fixes on someone else just as my faculty of thought does. And once it does, it most often compartmentalizes and forgets that person. As Weil notes, pity is unlike compassion in that "it consists in helping someone in misfortune so as not to be obliged to think about him anymore, or for the pleasure of feeling the distance between him and oneself."[20]

Compassion, in contrast, means that I identify with the afflicted individual so fully that I feed him for the same reason I feed myself: because we are both hungry. In other words, I have paid him attention. It is a faculty that does not latch onto the other, but instead remains still and open. We do not fully understand a hammer, Martin Heidegger observed, simply by staring at it. Instead, understanding comes when we pick it up and use it. Weil gives this observation an unusual wrinkle: we do not fully understand a fellow human being by staring, thinking, or even commiserating with her. Instead, understanding comes only when we let go of our self and allow the other to grab our full attention. In order for the reality of the other's self to fully invest us, we must first divest ourselves of our own selves.

It is tempting to see this faculty as thinking about thinking, or what psychologists call metacognition. This approach, at first glance, bears a resemblance to the meditation and mindfulness courses that are now multiplying at colleges and universities. One institution of higher learning, Lesley University, now offers a master's degree in mindfulness studies, while academics can join professional organizations like the Center for Contemplative Mind in Society, which seeks "to transform higher education by supporting and encouraging the use of contemplative/introspective practices and perspectives." These programs seek to develop what the psychologist Tobin Hart describes as "knowing through silence, looking inward, pondering deeply, beholding, witnessing the contents of our consciousness."

At first glance, this seems to be what Weil meant. Citing Descartes, she told Anne Reynaud and her fellow students that it "is one thing to be conscious, quite another to be conscious that one is."[21] But the resemblance ends here. Weil's philosophical stance does not call upon her students to look inward and consider the contents of their consciousness. To the contrary, Weil urges them to look outward and away from the contents of their consciousness. Being conscious of our consciousness is a starting point, not an end point, meta- or otherwise. "Complete attention," Weil declared, "is like unconsciousness." As such, it is a state that does not entail a particular action or stance, but instead suggests a form of reception, open and nonjudgmental, of the world. In a beautifully evocative phrase, Weil writes that when we translate a text from a foreign language into our own, we rightly do not seek to add anything to it. Ideally, this is how the student must approach the world. She must see and write about it as if she is translating "a text that is not written down." In an age where students cannot escape their social media shadows, this is less a Zen riddle than a pedagogical urgency.

Such a state is difficult to reach, much less to grade. Reynaud would not have been surprised to learn of her former teacher's exhortation, made several years later, that students must "work without any wish to gain good marks, to pass examinations, to win school successes; without any reference to their natural abilities and tastes; applying themselves equally to all their tasks, with the idea that each one will help to form in them the habit of attention." One might as well flunk a new student of basketball who, though absorbed by the exercise, fails to hit the rim with his shots. "Every time that a human being succeeds in making an effort of attention with the sole idea of increasing his grasp of truth, he acquires a greater aptitude for grasping it, even if his effort produces no visible fruit."[22]

Weil's portrayal of attention has been said to resemble the *vita contemplativa* traditionally associated with ancient thinkers from Plato to Augustine.[23] But the resemblance is potentially misleading, if only because we usually assume the contemplative life is the same as a passive life—a life in which the highest good seems to entail the abandonment of practical engagement in the world. But Weilian attention leads its practitioner precisely back into the thick of the world. Paying attention to others means that I must acknowledge and respect their reality. As we belong to the same world and are equally vulnerable to the crushing reality of force, I reorient my attention to them and away from myself. Peter Winch memorably captured this condition: "I cannot understand the other's affliction from the point of view of my own privileged position; I have rather to understand myself from the standpoint of the other's affliction, to understand that my privileged position is not part of my essential nature, but an accident of fate."[24]

‹‹›

What if we were to see the act of attention as a spiritual exercise? In a series of books, Pierre Hadot, the renowned historian of ancient philosophy, revealed that philosophy isn't what it used to be—or, at least, what it was in antiquity. Rather than constituting a discipline devoted to constructing systems of abstract or logical claims about the world, ancient philosophies offered various practices, what Hadot calls "spiritual exercises," meant to change the way in which one saw the world, and thus change one's own self. By joining a school of philosophy—Epicurean or Stoic, Platonist or Aristotelian—novices sought, not to master physics or metaphysics, ethics or logic, but instead to remaster their own character. The decision to join a particular school was more than an intellectual choice; it was, in a fundamental sense, an existential choice. How could it be otherwise, when the goal of ancient philosophy was not to inform, but instead to *form* the individual? Philosophy, at least in Hadot's reconstruction, thus rediscovers its original purpose: it is a discipline, or spiritual exercise, that trains your character to mesh with a set of moral principles. As one climbs the ladder of these exercises, which varied from school to school, the distance between words and acts shrinks and, at the last rung, meshes perfectly in the person of a true sage. From this perspective, the ancient works assume a radically new character. Rather than texts meant to fill the student's head, they are tools meant to sculpt the self.[25]

For Hadot, Marcus Aurelius's *Meditations* is a notebook that the Roman emperor filled with reminders and reflections, exhortations and exercises meant to keep him on the Stoic straight and narrow. Weil's notebooks, in contrast, served several purposes; as Richard Rees pointed out, there is "probably not a single fundamental problem of our age, in any domain, that is not resolutely faced and examined somewhere in these pages."[26] Weil's journal entries, couched in clear and strong handwriting that runs across dozens of the *cahiers*, the notebooks used by French students, are overwhelmingly weighted toward the last years of her life. The years of exile, between 1940 and 1943, contain more than nine-tenths of her private writings, and it is as if the convulsive character of this period left its mark on the physical character of the notebooks. Weil would frequently tear out and rearrange pages, while on other pages she wrote quite literally against the grain by juxtaposing vertical columns alongside horizontal entries. Dozens of passages are in Sanskrit, Greek, and Latin, while yet others are devoted to mathematical equations and geometrical diagrams; many entries are cryptic—hardly surprising for a private journal— while many others, no less unsurprisingly, are aphoristic.

What is *not* found in these pages impresses us as much as what *is* found. Weil never meant for her journals to be read by others, much less published, yet she almost never refers to private events in her life. The pages are barren of anecdotal accounts and private feelings; thoughts concerning family and friends, desires and dreams, past or present almost never surface. This silence is not due to a kind of *pudeur*, or reticence about personal matters, since Weil also rarely refers to political or practical matters, despite living in an era when the battering of force had never seemed more brutal and relentless. Were the journals to be opened today by someone who knew nothing of twentieth-century history, they would be none the wiser upon closing them.

The same, though, could be said of Marcus Aurelius's *Meditations*. In these pages, the history of Rome and the decisions made by the man who ruled over it are pushed beyond the margins. The *Meditations*, like the notebooks, are meant not to engage the world, but instead to engage the self. To this degree, Weil shares Marcus Aurelius's method and goal: she keeps a running account of her own spiritual exercises in order to remake herself. She berates herself for falling short of a goal or failing to grasp a clue, declaring, "I'm stupid . . . An example of my stupidity. Analyze it."[27] Thus the reminder to herself that at "every blow of fate, every pain, whether small or great, say to oneself: 'I am being worked on.'"[28] In one of her earliest entries, made in 1933 or 1934 when she was teaching in Roanne, she declares: "At the age of 25, it is time to finish once and for all with childhood." Around the same time, she makes a "list of temptations (to be read every morning)."[29] Chief among the temptations identified by the twenty-four-year-old Weil—who, we must not forget, was then dividing her time between teaching her *lycée* students and commuting on weekends to Saint-Étienne to teach workers and join union activities, all the while writing for various syndicalist and anarchist papers—was that of idleness. While this might strike the reader as perverse—aptly, the "temptation of perversity" is last on Weil's list—it nevertheless reflects her preoccupation with attending to the world. "Never surrender to the flow of time," she exhorts herself, and "allow yourself only those feelings which are actually called upon for effective use or else are required by thought for the sake of inspiration."[30]

In this call for adjusting one's thoughts and activities to worldly constraints, Weil even cites Marcus Aurelius: "The man who thinks he is ruled by a capricious nature is a slave, and the man who knows he is ruled by a nature determined by rigorous laws is a citizen of the world."[31] Hence the capital distinction she makes concerning the use of method: "What is important (for freedom) is not that the work should be methodical, but that it should be *methodically performed*."[32] Time and again, she focuses on the relentlessness of time and the necessity of starting again. "*Never* put something off indefinitely, but only to a definitely fixed time. Try to do this even when it is impossible (headaches . . .) Exercises: decide to do something, no matter what, and do it *exactly* at a certain time."[33]

Nowhere was methodical exercise more central than in Weil's notion of attention—a concern that Marcus Aurelius did not share. To observe the world rightly requires much practice, in part because the observer must overcome her own selfish reflexes. This is especially true when it comes to gazing upon instances of *malheur*. "To contemplate what cannot be contemplated (the affliction of another), without running away," Weil writes, "and to contemplate the desirable without approaching—that is what is beautiful."[34] Returning to this theme several pages later, she notes that true contemplation allows her to see others "as they are related to themselves, and not to me."[35] The ethical implications of this kind of sight—a way of seeing that is divorced from the concerns of the seer—are momentous.

As with any form of exercise that aims to train and strengthen, the proper exercise of our faculty of attention requires resistance. It is like an obstacle course we are asked to run, but it is a peculiar kind of course. Not only are the obstacles our fellow human beings, but they are also obstacles we have spent our lives learning *not* to see. When we encounter such obstacles, our reflex is to see right through them—that is, we see right through them if they are deprived of the ability to insist upon being seen. We must see them as they see themselves: not as means to a particular end, but as ends in and of themselves. As a result, just as we know that there are actions we can undertake, there are others we know—better yet, *see*—that we cannot undertake because the obstacles are all too human. In her essay on the *Iliad*, Weil depicts Achilles as seeing through Priam. The father of the slain Hector, Priam has become a supplicant, unable to refuse or resist in his desire to recover his son's body.

It is when Achilles contemplates the image of his own father, Peleus, who will one day grieve his own son's death, that he can no longer dismiss Priam's humanity. He feeds and shelters the old man—in effect, he fully *sees* him—after they weep together. Mere mortals, Weil makes clear in another essay, are no different in this regard: "Anything within the field of action which does not constitute an obstacle—as, for instance, men deprived of the power to refuse—is transparent for thought in the way completely clear glass is for sight. It has no power to stop, just as our eyes have no power to see the glass."[36] In the end, the proper use of attention allows one to see, but not see through, the clear glass panes that fill our world.

⁑

Though it is a word now rarely heard outside of places of worship, "reverence" also captures Weil's notion of attention. It is a quality shared by one of the philosophers whose work she taught to her students, Immanuel Kant. Most famously, in his *Groundwork of the Metaphysics of Morals*, Kant approaches the state of reverence through the notion of *Achtung*. It is the sensation we experience upon registering—getting knocked across the head by, really—the force of moral law or, better yet, its embodiment in a particular human being. There are times when, sleepwalking through our lives, we snap to attention upon seeing a fellow human being act on a maxim they believe—indeed, that they *know*—applies to all men and women. There are moments when another's gesture or word marks our lives; it commands our respect; it demands our reverence. The presence of *Achtung*, Kant writes, makes us of "worthy of humanity." We make ourselves worthy by acknowledging the dignity of humanity in every other human being. This entails, Kant states, "the reverence [*Achtung*] that must be shown to each and every one."[37]

Reverence is the work of attention. In fact, reverence *is*

attention. Not the poised attention taught in hospitality studies: the eager smile, bracketed gaze, and predictable warmth
of a hotel receptionist. Attention, in such instances, is attending to the appearance of attention—which is probably a good
thing if all you expect is to be asked for a room key. Instead, as
Weil declares, attention is "the rarest and purest form of generosity." The act of giving oneself—turning away from one's own
self and turning toward the world, making a place for others by
placing one's own self in a subordinate position—is true attention. Attentiveness entails the difficult task of waiting, not for
the world to take note of us, but for us to take note of the world.
We take our seat in the world's *salle d'attente*, forget our own
itinerary, and open ourselves to the itineraries of others. It is
the realization that we are not alone, the realization that we can
never allow ourselves to believe we are alone, the realization that
we all too easily confuse the world that is as it is for a world that
is all about us. By attending to the world, we open ourselves to
the awe, secular no less than religious, that we experience upon
confronting things greater and deeper than us, and the sense
of humility that follows. Reverence, in short, is the realization
that there is more than this and that there is more than me; it
is both the cause and consequence, as Iris Murdoch notes, of
"the extremely difficult realization that something other than
oneself is real."

⁎⁎

It is difficult to realize that even the powerful are real. In her
essay on the right use of school studies, Weil makes mention of
a Grail legend. Guarding the holy object, Weil notes, is a king
partly paralyzed by a terrible wound. He will give the Grail to
the first seeker who, rather than asking for the object, instead
asks the king, "What are you going through?" This seeker does
not relegate the king to the category of "unfortunates"—even of

the royal variety—but instead sees him "as a man, exactly like us, who was one day stamped with a special mark by affliction." For this reason, we must "know how to look at him in a certain way"—in a word, attentively.[38]

At times, this passage comes to my mind when I am driving to work. Interstate 45, the concrete Nile that slices north to south through Houston, is generally not a place for moral quandaries. That is, until you exit, stop at the first intersection, and confront an ethical impasse at the underpass. There, at the red light, I often face a panhandler. *Face*: there is no better verb, if only because it is also the noun that captures what is truly at stake. Many of us do our very best to evade these face-offs. There are drivers who, coming to a stop next to the panhandler, will nudge their cars forward; others will try to edge their way into the left lane. Still other drivers will run the light—and run the risk of an accident—in order, or so I suspect, to avoid spending the next several seconds in the company of the panhandler. When those options fail us, there are yet other strategies. Some of us stare furiously at our smartphones or our radios, while others take a newfound interest in our odometer readings. Many of us will gaze straight ahead pretending to be lost in thought, all the while a prisoner of just one thought: why is the light taking so long to turn green?

Some of us will look at the panhandler, but as we might look at faces in a police lineup, or at X-rays of our children's teeth. We try to assess their situation, comparing the pleas on their signs with the clothing on their bodies or expressions on their faces. Aren't those Ray-Bans he's wearing? if he's really homeless, why is he so clean-shaven? why is the dog lying so quietly at his feet? Or: Is she drugged? and if she is feeding three kids, why is she overweight? Or: No wonder they are begging for money, they clearly spent their last penny on their tattoos.

How do I know about all of these tactics, ruses, and excuses?

It's simple: I've tried them all. While I may send out yearly checks to a dozen charities, I cannot without effort fork over to a man holding a sign the couple of bucks I would thoughtlessly spend on an espresso. Why? In *The Brothers Karamazov*, one of Fyodor Dostoyevsky's characters declares that while we might love our neighbor abstractly, we rarely do so up close. This is why, he concludes, beggars "should never show themselves in the street." This is certainly the case on the feeder roads to I-45. Unlike the downtown sidewalks or parks, the rebar-reinforced banks along the macadam tributaries of I-45 are the last place one expects to face a face. In these parts encountering another human being who isn't enveloped in a steel and glass shell is always a bit of a shock.

And yet, there she is, a human being, her head abuzz with the torrent of traffic as she slowly works the line of cars. She is carrying a sign—black marks scrawled across the side of a cardboard box—that announces she is willing to accept any kind of handout and offer God's blessing. Her cheeks are livid, her hair is unwashed, her eyes move steadily from one idling car to the next. Let's face it: she wants to be seen. Will I, though, allow myself to see her? Or will I allow the inevitable bottleneck of questions and rationalizations to come in between us? Like the common wisdom that panhandlers will spend my buck on drugs or booze, the common tale of beggars driving off in a Mercedes once their work shift is over, and the common fear that they carry exotic diseases.

But where is my common sense in all of this? Must we be sociologists to know that most panhandlers in fact spend their money on food? Does one need to be an economist to know that giving cash to the poor is the most efficient way to help them? Should one even think of these afflicted individuals as categories or types? Weil warns against seeing our fellow human beings as anything other than human beings. "I see a passerby in the street," she writes, who "has long arms, blue eyes, and a mind whose thoughts I do not know, but perhaps they are commonplace."

Paradoxically, these details are crucial because they are inconsequential. They are not what makes this particular passerby irreplaceable or, to use Weil's term, "sacred." Instead, it is his whole person. He is no more a stand-in for a particular group of human beings than is the man—and not the panhandler—at the Clear Lake City Boulevard exit who wears a grayish tank top and a Houston Astros cap at a rakish slant, and whose thoughts I do not know. I repeat the lines from "Human Personality"—"It is this man; no more and no less . . . which is sacred to me"[39] —and, at the same time, recall the warning from "The Love of God and Affliction" that we "can only accept the existence of affliction by considering it at a distance."[40] As for accepting the existence of affliction from a few feet away and on the other side of a car window, it takes a miracle. Or, at least, it takes someone more prone to miracles than I am. When I do open the window, it is often because one of my children is also in the car, and I wish to set a model, or (more shamefully) wish them to think I am a better person than I actually am.

This is, of course, a pathetic and paltry, self-centered and shameless motivation. But it is not utterly inconsequential—at least if one of my children, or another driver, is paying even a modicum of attention to the exchange. I am not sure if Weil would approve, but Murdoch, once again, might be less severe. She notes that all of us are "naturally attached" to those things we find valuable. Those attachments are formed with fellow men and women, as well as with certain cultural and social practices and values that orient our vision in certain ways. Our ability to see grows over the course of our lives, and, as Weil and Murdoch both insist, seeing is doing. "There is nothing odd or mystical about this, nor about the fact that our ability to act well 'when the time comes' depends partly, perhaps largely, upon the quality of our habitual objects of attention."[41] I don't know if one of my children will, one day, open the car window, look at the man or woman standing by the light, and, as Weil would have us do, ask him: "What are you going through?"[42] I don't know if I, not to mention my children, will ever do this. But I do know the question is important, and I want my children to know this as well. Our sight may never be as clear as we wish, but at least we will never mistake our moral astigmatism for clear vision.

CHAPTER THREE

The Varieties of Resistance

Even if defeat is inevitable, I will always choose to side with the
vanquished workers than the victorious oppressors.
SIMONE WEIL

I rebel—therefore we exist.
ALBERT CAMUS

In 1938, Weil wrote a fan letter to one of France's best known
writers and intellectuals, Georges Bernanos. At first glance, this
was an odd gesture. While Bernanos's militant Catholicism and
deep-seated anti-Semitism would not necessarily have repelled
Weil, his ardent monarchism and Francoism should have. This
perhaps explains why Weil shared a bit of her own background
with Bernanos. "From my childhood onwards," she explained,
"I sympathized with those organizations which spring from the
lowest and least regarded social strata." And yet, though she and
the fiercely conservative Bernanos did not share the same ideology, Weil nevertheless sensed they shared this same attitude
toward those who have little or nothing. For this reason, she
concluded, no matter how "silly it may be to write to an author,
I cannot refrain from doing so."[1]

Indeed, how could Weil refrain? She had just read Bernanos's *Les Grands cimetières sous la lune*, his blistering personal account of the Spanish Civil War, in which he savaged his
fellow conservatives as mercilessly as he did the Spanish and
French revolutionaries. The devout Bernanos, however, saved

his greatest scorn for the Spanish clergy. In one episode, he tells how a few priests carefully went about their clerical duties, absolving a group of Catalan prisoners taken by Franco's soldiers. They then looked on as the soldiers who had captured the prisoners "unhurriedly shot *les malheureux* one by one," poured gasoline over their remains, and set them on fire. The next day, Bernanos saw "these blackened and shining men, twisted by the flames, some of them in positions obscene enough to afflict their confessors."[2]

These descriptions shocked Weil, but they did not surprise her. "I have had," she explained, "an experience which corresponds to your own." But it was an experience, she added, "much shorter and less profound." In July 1936, shortly after the initial uprising of the Falangist movement, led by General Francisco Franco, Weil decided her place was beside those defending the Spanish Republic. Deeply sympathetic with the anarchist and syndicalist movements in France, Weil traveled to Barcelona and tried, without success, to enlist in the Trotskyist party in Spain, the POUM, which George Orwell would join at year's end. The POUM's leadership was no doubt put off by Weil's insistent requests to be sent behind enemy lines in order to recruit women to fight against Franco's forces. The preposterousness of her plan and inadequacy of her command of Spanish were seen as serious handicaps by everyone except her.[3] Undeterred, Weil then embedded herself, under the guise of a journalist, in the militia of the National Labor Confederation (CNT), a labor organization with strong anarcho-syndicalist leanings.

Weil soon peeled off from the other journalists, attaching herself to a small group of foreign fighters who were part of a militia preparing to march to the battlefront along the Ebre River. Known as the Durruti Column, the militia was named after its commander, the fiery Catalan anarchist Buenaventura Durruti. A foe of both the monarchy and republic, Durruti had been in hiding in Barcelona when the civil war erupted. His rapid organization of the local workers to oppose Franco's forces was aided by his soaring oratory: "We are not in the least afraid of ruins . . . We are going to inherit the earth . . . We carry a new world in our hearts, a world that is growing at this very moment."[4] But to bring this new world into being, Durruti was willing to sacrifice those he assigned to the old world. He was a ruthless leader who did not hesitate to kill prisoners whom he conveniently labeled as "fascists," regardless of their political affiliation.[5]

Having lived by the sword, Durruti died by it in November 1936, cut down by Franco's forces during a street battle in Madrid. By then, Weil had safely returned to France, but only at the end of a series of tragi-comic events. On August 17, her motley platoon reached the town of Pina, a republican stronghold near the front. She reported to a friend that when she saw an enemy plane drop a bomb, and heard the distant explosion that followed, she was "not at all disturbed."[6] But this was decidedly not her fellow militants' reaction during sessions of practice shooting. Tutored by a French volunteer in the basics of gunmanship, Weil, with her poor eyesight and physical awkwardness, made a hopeless student. Whenever she shouldered her rifle, her fellow soldiers gave Weil wide berth. As she reassured her friend Simone Pétrement, "Happily, I am so myopic that there's no risk of my killing others, even when I am aiming at them."[7]

Fatefully, her myopia brought an early end to her time as a combatant. On the morning of August 20, scarcely three days after she arrived at the front, Weil stumbled into a large pot of boiling oil that the platoon's cook had placed on the ground. While her shoe protected her foot, the bottom part of her leg was severely burned. When Weil was carried to a makeshift hospital in Pina, the chief medical officer gave her a purge to drink and directed her to get up and walk, using her leg, for twenty minutes. Mystified by the doctor's prescription, Weil learned that he had been a hairstylist before the war. As a result, Weil made her way to Barcelona, where her mother and father met her. Once again unable to find adequate care for her festering wound, she and her parents continued north to Sitgès, near the French border. After long resisting her parents' insistent pleas to return to Paris, Weil reluctantly agreed; on September 25, parents and daughter crossed the border back into France.

By then, though, Weil learned that her literal misstep had, in fact, saved her life. While she was convalescing in Sitgès, Weil's platoon suffered a bloody defeat in a battle near the town of Perdiguera. Among the dozens of dead, it turns out, were several women who had joined the group after Weil's forced departure from the front. At Sitgès, she also learned that her own side had committed a war atrocity just outside town. Following a failed attack that resulted in nine deaths, the republican militia exacted revenge by shooting in cold blood nine local youths whom they had accused, with no evidence, of being fascists. Recounting this episode in her letter to Bernanos, Weil offered a bleak observation: "Never once, either among Spaniards or even among the French who were in Spain as combatants or as visitors—the latter being usually dim and harmless intellectuals—never once did I hear anyone express, even in private intimacy, any repulsion or disgust or even disapproval of useless bloodshed."[8]

In *Homage to Catalonia*, Orwell recalls a telling episode while he fought alongside the anarchists in Spain. On a reconnaissance mission with a fellow soldier near Huesca, he caught sight of an enemy soldier who, startled by the sound of airplanes, leaped from the trench where he had been busy defecating. "He was half-dressed and holding up his trousers with both hands as he ran. I refrained from shooting him." Asking himself why, he found that his answer was simple: "I had come here to shoot at 'Fascists,' but a man who is holding up his trousers is not a 'Fascist,' he is visibly a fellow creature, similar to yourself, and you do not feel like shooting at him."[9] At this moment, Orwell resisted a feeling that even Weil found overwhelming, what she called the "sort of intoxication" that affects human beings when they learn they can "kill without fear of punishment or blame." In a letter to Father Perrin, she confided her own inability to resist the madness of war: "I was horrified, but not surprised by the war crimes. I felt the possibility of doing the same—and it's precisely because I felt that potential that I was horrified."[10]

Her accident, and subsequent convalescence, cut short Weil's prolonged exposure to the madness of war. Even so, Weil insisted upon assuming responsibility, and the accompanying guilt, for her participation. Taking cover when an enemy plane flew overhead, Weil stretched out on the ground, stared at the sky, and told herself: "If they [the Franquists] take me, they will kill me. But it will be deserved. Our side has spilled enough blood. I am morally complicit."[11] Yet Weil's sense of moral complicity in the death of others had also led her to join the war in the first place. As she told Bernanos, the fact that she had already, when still in Paris, taken sides in Spain's civil war meant that she could not remain safely in France. As a committed pacifist, she found this a particularly difficult decision. "I do not love war," she explained, "but what has always seemed to me most horrible in war is the position of those in the rear."[12] In other words, what was most horrible was less the refusal to make moral choices than the knowing assumption of the existential risks they necessarily entail.

For Orwell, all the talk about bloodshed in Spain on behalf of democracy "was plain eye-wash." There was no one, he concluded, "who spent more than a few weeks in Spain without being in some degree disillusioned." He dismissed Franco as an "anachronism," but also slammed the Popular Front as a "swindle." Still, Orwell preferred the republican swindle to the fascist anachronism.[13] Weil was equally dry-eyed about her own side's lack of innocence. But she was no less certain that she had to choose, and that choosing entailed resistance. To do anything less was a betrayal of oneself and one's fellow human beings. As she had told her students in Roanne at the end of a lecture on French economic policies, and their consequences for the working class: "If one stops oneself from thinking of all this, one makes oneself an accomplice of what is happening. One has to do something quite different: take one's place in this system of things and do something about it."[14]

⁂

The verb "resist" derives from the Latin *stare*, "to stand." At a fundamental level, resistance is a universal activity: all living organisms struggle to remain standing, if only figuratively, as long as possible. It is a reflexive, not reflective, act. This is as true for moss and millipedes as for oaks and us. But when reflection enters the scene, as it does with humans, the meaning of "resist" ramifies in all sorts of directions.

For the sake of self-survival, our resistance is instinctual; for the sake of self-mastery, however, our resistance must become counter-instinctual. Various schools of ancient philosophy, from the Stoics to the Epicureans, taught their followers to resist recklessness and rationales; to resist panic and passion; to resist controlling others and resist losing control of themselves. Such resistance affirms that the truly free individual is one who takes the world as it is and aligns with it as best they can.

Yet resistance in both of the preceding senses—the struggle against external and internal forces—does not make our lives worth living. A worthwhile life accepts and acts on a core number of moral ideals: the primacy of justice and truth, the pursuit of happiness and goodness, the preeminence of the dignity and humanity of each and every human being. In effect, a life worth living is a life devoted to "doing something about it."

Even as a child, as we saw, Weil insisted on doing something. Weil's revolutionary engagement deepened once she began studies at the Lycée Henri IV, which overlooks the Left Bank from the top of the steep hill known as the Montagne Sainte Geneviève. It was at Henri IV that she met Émile Chartier, the philosophy professor who became one of the greatest influences on her intellectual life. Known to the public by his penname, Alain, Chartier was a prolific writer whose defiance of state institutions, disdain for organized religion, and devotion to republican values embodied, for better and for worse, the ethos of late nineteenth-century France. Though old enough to avoid the draft, and educated enough to become an officer, Chartier served with the artillery during World War I, refusing promotions that would have removed him from active duty. Though he survived the war with a leg wound, the experience shattered whatever illusions he had about the reach of reason, as well as any reasons to trust the nation's political leaders. Chartier became a militant pacifist and severe skeptic of political parties and their leaders, whether they were on the left or the right. In his essays—short meditations he called *propos*—he warned his readers to distrust those promising salvation through either revolution or reaction. Instead, as an admirer of Plato and Kant, Chartier insisted upon two crucial virtues for the health of civil society: obedience and resistance. Without the former, society risks anarchy; without the latter, it invites tyranny. Order would collapse without the presence of obedience, yet liberty would wither without the spirit of resistance. Nevertheless, when he weighs one against the other, Alain places his finger on the scale of resistance. The ideal citizen, he declared, must "remain inflexible, defiant, and suspicious of those in power."[15]

Chartier left his mark on the several generations of men and women who entered his classroom. As if underscoring his exhortation that life had to be lived standing up, he would pace with a limp across the front of the room while lecturing, using the same direct language, as free of philosophical jargon and rhetorical excess as were his *propos*. Along with entire texts from Plato and Kant, Chartier also assigned Spinoza and Marcus Aurelius to his students—thinkers who, though in very different ways and words, emphasized our freedom to think and our duty to act as moral agents. Though there was little flash or drama to his nonconformism, Chartier's example deeply impressed his students. When warned by his administrators that the next generation would be difficult to control, he replied: "I very much hope so."

Those same qualities of intellectual freedom and moral duty were already rooted in Weil's character when she entered his classroom, but Chartier cultivated them with particular care. Impressed by his pupil's remarkable character—"she was so different from the rest of us," he observed, "and judged us with supreme independence"—Chartier fondly referred to Weil as "the Martian."[16] He was struck, in particular, by the mixture of intellectual rigor and moral clarity he found in Weil's writings. One of her essays, devoted to the question of beauty and goodness, earned a rare comment of "*très beau*" from her teacher. In the essay, Weil describes a famous gesture made by Alexander the Great while marching with his soldiers across the desert: when offered a goblet of water, he emptied it on the sand, thus expressing his solidarity with the parched soldiers. The moral, for Weil, was clear: "if he had accepted to drink the water, he would have set himself apart from his soldiers . . . Sacrifice is the acceptance of pain, the refusal to obey one's animal needs and the will to redeem the suffering of others by choosing to suffer as well."[17] Weil thus reveals the similarity between Chartier's practice of philosophy and her own: one freely chooses to obey the call of goodness, an act that originates in the self and ripples across the world.

⁂

Upon her graduation from the Lycée Henri IV—an event crowned by Chartier's parting observation that she was destined to enjoy "brilliant success"—Weil became the only female student in the entering class of 1928 at the École Normale Supérieure, the nation's hothouse for its brightest students.[18] While Chartier had admired Weil's unwavering intellectual and moral stance, the staff at the ENS were less impressed. They were outraged by her indifference to her clothing—she invariably wore flat shoes and a long skirt with a masculine cut, and she refused to don a hat (more or less *de rigueur* for bourgeois women at the time)—and disturbed by her refusal to abide by the school's traditions. When she violated the rule forbidding female students from smoking in the same courtyard with the male students, the director, Célestin Bouglé, expelled her for a week. Rather than a badge of shame, the young Weil wore the punishment as a medal of honor, boasting of her achievement to her resigned parents when she triumphantly returned home that night.[19]

Fellow students were also often bewildered by the blistering intensity of their classmate's political and social commitments. Some found her impossible to digest, others found her impossible to understand. In her *Memoirs of a Dutiful Daughter*, Simone de Beauvoir recalled her first and, it turned out, last conversation with Weil. Hearing the stories circulating about Weil—most famously, when she burst into tears upon learning of a famine ravaging China—Beauvoir was eager to meet her fellow philosophy student. When she finally did, the meeting did not last long. After brief introductions, Beauvoir must have touched on the Chinese famine, because Weil peremptorily announced that "one thing alone mattered in the world today: The Revolution that would feed all the people on the earth." When Beauvoir demurred, suggesting that the point to life was to find, not happiness, but meaning, Weil cut her short: "It's easy to see you've never gone hungry."[20]

At the ENS, Weil's political engagement intensified, though it multiplied rather than deepened. She persisted in her provocations of the school administration, aiming much of her disdain at the long-suffering Bouglé. Revealing a streak of cruelty, Weil once approached Bouglé for a donation to a fund for the unemployed. Wishing to avoid publicity, Bouglé gave Weil 20 francs, but requested anonymity for his gift. Weil, however, refused to grant her nemesis his wish. On flyers posted shortly after in the school's hallways, students and faculty were exhorted to donate: "Follow the example of your director. Give anonymously to the Unemployed Fund."[21]

The wounded Bouglé muttered that the recalcitrant student was spending her time organizing for "*le Grand Soir*"—slang for "the Revolution."[22] But Bouglé was blind to the difference in the shades of red between the political views espoused by Weil and those of the French Communist Party (PCF). At this stage of her evolution, Weil was certainly a revolutionary, but not the sort who applied for membership in the PCF. Even as an idealistic youth, she never joined the party, as did so many of her contemporaries. In fact, like Chartier, Weil was by nature suspicious of all political parties. Regardless of their ideological bent, political leaders sought power; power, in turn, sooner or later transformed them into oppressors. Moreover, Weil had few illusions about the independence of mind and action of the leaders of the PCF, who were taking their marching orders from Moscow. Rather like a faithful Christian who does not belong to a church, or a practicing Jew who never sets foot in a temple, the young Weil considered herself a communist with a small *c*.

It was the only ideology that sought to defend the rights of the dispossessed and desperate, workers and those who could not find work at all. Tellingly, she fell into the habit of adorning her sheets of classroom notes with hammers and sickles.[23]

The problem with Marxism is that it ignores the lived experience of workers. Marxist theorists, Weil observed, were in no position to expound on worker alienation when "they themselves have never been cogs in the machinery of factory."[24] This is the reason why, after she had begun working at Alsthom, she could tell a former student that she had "the impression of having escaped from a world of abstractions."[25] The numbing repetition of tasks, deafening roar of engines, and unending terror of unemployment were, paradoxically, reminders of life. Truth itself must be rooted in the world of experience, not theory. Truth, she always insisted, must be rescued from pure speculation. Instead, truth is "always a truth about something."[26]

Long before Alsthom, Weil was already in search of similar experiences, determined to locate truths in the rhythm of everyday life. During the summer vacation before her last year at the École Normale Supérieure, in 1931, Weil asked several fishermen in the Norman village where she was staying if she could work on their boats. No doubt baffled by the request from this bourgeois Parisienne, or perhaps bothered by the rumor that she was a communist, all the fishermen but one turned her down. The exception was Marcel Lecarpentier who, though surprised by the request, also sensed the remarkable nature of the woman who made it. Indifferent to the rumors that Weil was a communist, Lecarpentier allowed Weil to join him and his brother on their trawler. Though irremediably maladroit in her assigned tasks, Weil worked tirelessly and without complaint or fear. During a night expedition, the trawler was caught in a storm, and the anxious Lecarpentier told Weil she needed to be tied down for her safety. His frail passenger refused, telling him she was not afraid to die: "I've always done my duty."[27]

This reply sounds melodramatic; perhaps it *was* melodramatic. Nevertheless, it contains an important truth. "Duty" was, in effect, a four-letter word for "engagement." And engagement was a two-way street. Along with Weil's efforts to learn about the world of physical labor were her attempts to give workers lessons from the world into which she had been born. When not unraveling nets on board Lecarpentier's boat, Weil tutored him in math and literature. Even after she returned to Paris, she continued to send Lecarpentier books to read, and had him send her his own work so she could read and correct it. "She wanted to know our misery," Lecarpentier recalled, but she "also wanted to free the worker."[28]

With a determination that either attracted or alienated those with whom she came into contact, Weil pursued this goal. During the years she spent as a teacher, Weil was no less determined to connect with local workers than with her students. In fact, the two often became one and the same. Soon after she arrived in Le Puy, Weil contacted Urbain Thévenon, a teacher in the nearby mining city of Saint-Étienne, who had founded a night school for workers. Their first encounter was not promising. Calling unannounced at the teacher's apartment, Weil was met at the door by Thévenon's wife, Albertine. Not bothering to greet Mme. Thévenon, Weil abruptly demanded to know if her husband was home, then strode past the startled woman without waiting for a reply.

Despite this unlikely start, the three soon became close friends, with Weil making the three-hour train ride from Le Puy at least once a week in order to teach at Thévenon's school. In her classes, devoted to the French language and political economy, Weil sought to give her blue-collar students the means to share what she insisted was the "heritage of human culture." Rather than ignore or scorn this heritage, workers must instead make it their own: to take possession of this cultural legacy was itself a revolutionary act. But, as her colleagues, if not her students, were discovering, Weil had a fundamentally conservative, if not reactionary, conception of "revolution" and "resistance."

⁎

A radical notion lies at the heart—or, more accurately, at the *root*—of Weil's conception of teaching. To teach is to awaken those who had, in John Stuart Mill's phrase, fallen into "the deep slumber of decided opinion." Or, even more desperately, those who had been buried alive, effectively transformed into things by the combined forces of mechanization, industrialization, and bureaucratization. In her early essay "Reflections concerning the Causes of Liberty and Social Oppression," Weil dwells on the practical difficulties involved in this pedagogical effort. Thought, which she describes as "man's supreme dignity," is difficult to practice in a world given over to the "collectivity."[29]

"Collectivity" is an unsettling word. On first hearing, it brings to mind films, such as *The Matrix* or *The Circle*, that depict organizations or systems with occult powers and vast reach. It certainly lends itself to the seemingly benign social media platforms, such as Facebook and Twitter, that now dominate our lives. But in her shifting descriptions of the notion, Weil warns that the "collectivity" is something both grander and grimmer. It is "completely abstract, wholly mysterious, inaccessible to the senses and to the mind." Odorless like a gas, the collectivity is also poisonous: "Never has the individual been so completely delivered up to a blind collectivity, and never have men been less capable, not only of subordinating their actions to their thought, but even of thinking."[30]

But Weil had in mind not just totalitarian states like Nazi

Germany and Communist Russia; she also had liberal societies in her sights. The meaning of "collectivity" tends to shift
from one text to the next, as does the word itself; at times, Weil
applies the label of "blind social mechanism." But the fundamental conception remains constant, pointing to the conver-
gence of the political, social, cultural, and economic forces that
dictate our lives. These forces hollow out language and darken
understanding, thus crippling our ability, in Weil's phrase, to
"come to grips" with the world. The idea of collectivity resembles Hannah Arendt's later notion of "thoughtlessness," the
condition she associated with Adolph Eichmann. In her controversial *Eichmann in Jerusalem: A Study in the Banality of Evil*,
Arendt argued that this Nazi bureaucrat shocks us not because
he was like Iago or Richard III, but because he was a mediocrity. "It was sheer thoughtlessness—something by no means
identical with stupidity—that predisposed him to become one
of the greatest criminals of that period."[31] Like so many of his
peers, Eichmann would not free himself, intellectually or morally, from the Nazi machine designed to induce inattention and
irresponsibility.

But the Nazis, as Weil and Arendt point out, did not have a
patent on such machines. Weil's factory experience taught her
that, among the toxins produced by modern industry, thoughtlessness was most dangerous. But it was not just factories that
manufactured this poison; nearly all organizations and institutions, by smothering the vital bond between language and meaning, make and keep us thoughtless. In a startling anticipation
of our own age, Weil declares: "With the popular press and the
wireless, you can make a whole people swallow with their break-
fast or supper a series of ready-made and, by the same token,
absurd opinions." As to whether these new forms of communication can be used for good, Weil's response is pitiless: "You
cannot with the aid of these things arouse so much as a gleam of

thought."[32] This is all the more true when these media become echo chambers for phrases and slogans that, devoid of tangible or verifiable content, obliterate the space or scope for thought. Whether they are chanted by French Communists of her era ("We are building a better future!") or by American Republicans of our era ("Make America Great Again!"), we confront the same phenomenon: the disemboweling of language and beggaring of thought.

This state of affairs is not surprising. Comforting beliefs, Weil noted, are seldom rational beliefs.[33] Like her ancient Stoics, however, Weil rejected this as a reason for resignation. Instead, she insisted upon the sovereignty of our minds. As she told her students at Roanne, the notion of "stoic resignation" was deeply misleading. Everything we do or say is rooted in our judgments, which in turn are under our control—that is, if we exercise the necessary discipline.[34] What she impressed upon the young women in her classes—"Every failure is lack of self-control"—is what she reminded the readers of the anarcho-syndicalist newspaper *La Révolution prolétarienne*: "Nothing in the world can prevent us from thinking clearly."[35]

Yet, for Weil, thinking is not necessarily liberating, at least in the usual sense of the word. No amount of sober and sustained thought can shield us from the overwhelming force that collectivities bring to bear on our lives, nor can it overcome the impossibility—or, perhaps, undesirability—of creating a world where work would no longer be necessary. Echoing Marcus Aurelius, Weil recognized that if we "were to understand by liberty the mere absence of necessity, the word would be emptied of all concrete meaning."[36] No matter how humane the intentions of an organization, no matter whether society is ordered on capitalist or socialist lines, oppression will not disappear. Oppression is nothing less than the sharp edge of force, and force is a natural, not social phenomenon. No less important, since force is inherently mercurial, always threatening to slip from the hands of oppressor to oppressed, "there is never power, but only a race for power."[37]

Although this conviction seems to lead us to despair, Weil insists it ought to spur us to resistance. We resist not in order to achieve everything we wish, but instead to achieve what we might reasonably expect. Herein lies one of her enduring insights: true resistance begins with clear thinking. As thinking creatures, we are incapable of accepting servitude. But true thinking cultivates moderation, not excess. "Perfect liberty is what we must try to represent clearly to ourselves, not in the hope of attaining a less imperfect liberty than is our present condition. The better can be conceived only by reference to the perfect."[38]

Once again revealing her intellectual debt to the Stoics, Weil offered what she called her "heroic conception" of liberty. By "heroic," she did not have in mind her childhood hero Cyrano de Bergerac. Instead, Weil was now thinking of Epictetus and Marcus Aurelius, for whom freedom can be achieved only by recognizing the forces at play in our lives and accepting the limits they impose upon us. True liberty, she argued, is defined "by a relationship between thought and action; the absolutely free man would be he whose every action proceeded from a preliminary judgment concerning the end which he set himself and the sequence of means suitable for attaining this end." Subject though we are to irresistible social, economic, and material forces, we can nevertheless assert our liberty by doing what we can within these constraints. "Man can choose between either blindly submitting to the spur with which necessity pricks him on from the outside, or else adapting himself to the inner representation of it that he forms in his own mind."[39]

Mindfulness, in essence, marks the crossroads between servitude and liberty. But such mindfulness entails effort, a sustained exertion to guard against the mindless phrases and slogans, opinions and beliefs that we too often confuse with the work of thinking. All too often, Weil observes, we say that force is powerless to overcome thought. But this very claim is thoughtless. For it to be true, she adds laconically, "there must be thought. Where irrational opinions hold the place of ideas, force is all-powerful."[40]

⁂

In *The Road to Wigan Pier*, his gripping account of the lot of miners in northern England, Orwell explained how mindfulness is especially elusive for these men. Descending a mine in Yorkshire, he noted the miners' bare torsos, carpeted in dust, always straining with effort; their careful drilling of holes into coal faces and placing of explosives designed to loosen the coal, but which could also bring down 400 feet of rock and dirt on their heads; their relentless shoveling of the black rubble onto a clattering and deafening conveyor belt. The product of a middle-class upbringing, Orwell found the experience revelatory. For his peers, it was easy to be oblivious to the lot of those who work with their hands. More so than anyone else, the miner stands for such a worker "not only because his work is so exaggeratedly awful, but also because it is so vitally necessary and yet so remote from our experience, so invisible, as it were, that we are capable of forgetting it as we forget the blood in our veins. In a way, it is even humiliating to watch coal miners working. It raises in you a momentary doubt about your own status as an 'intellectual' and a superior person generally."[41]

Remarkably, four years before Orwell arrived in Yorkshire, Weil had already made a descent into a mine pit. And, unlike Orwell, she had already long harbored doubts about her superiority. In 1932, while teaching in Le Puy, Weil persuaded a local mine owner, a friend of the Thévenons, to allow her to visit the site. But Weil refused to remain a mere observer. Upon reaching the bottom of the shaft, she asked a miner, just as she would turn to farmers and fishermen, to allow her to try out his tool. In this case, though, it was a heavy pneumatic drill. Cradling it against her chest, Weil could barely control the machine as it skipped across the coal face. Had not the miner reclaimed the drill, he later recalled, Weil would have continued drilling through sheer determination until her rattled body collapsed to the ground.[42]

Equally rattled were Weil's assumptions about the relationship between workers and their tools. The actual drama that unfolds underground is not between coal and man, she perceived, but instead between coal and compressed air. The drill was not designed to follow the body's natural rhythm; instead, the drill forces the body to adapt to its unnatural pace and power. Caught between these two forces—the coal face and the drill— the miner, now little more than an extension of the machine, is demolished a little more each day. Given this play of forces, Weil concluded, a political revolution would not change anything at all. What first needs to be addressed are the material conditions of work utterly changed by the technological revolution.[43]

Predictably, Weil asked to be hired full-time as a miner; predictably, the manager turned her down. Yet this did not dampen her efforts to slip into the world of manual labor. While she taught in Bourges, Weil repeatedly tried either to lose herself among the local workers or, conversely, to lead them in protest. Her efforts, however, veered between the comical and pitiful. Her attempt to persuade the puzzled waitresses at a local restaurant, for instance, that they were underpaid met with the protestations that they had everything they needed. Another day, while walking along a country lane, she persuaded a farmer to let her try his plow. She immediately overturned it, so upsetting the farmer that he refused Weil's peace offering of a cigarette.

Most telling, if only because the experience or, better yet, "experiment" lasted nearly a month, was Weil's relationship with the Belleville family. The Bellevilles, who lived on a small working farm outside Bourges, were related to one of Weil's students. At a meeting arranged by the student, Weil asked if she could move into their home. The husband and wife, surprised by the request, refused, but did agree to allow Weil to work on the farm.

They soon came to regret their decision. Weil plunged headfirst into the daily tasks at the farm, shoveling manure, digging for beets, and piling hay. Between her chores, she grilled the Bellevilles, asking them for details about the household economy or probing their thoughts about rural life. The couple realized that this strange young woman was unlike any other intellectual; as Mme. Belleville later observed, Weil "wanted to knock down the barriers and put herself at our level." The problem, though, was that the Bellevilles did not find that their level was as abysmally low as Weil found it. They were rightly annoyed by Weil's insistence on how unhappy and unrewarding their life was. When their guest told them that she wanted to "live the life of the poor, share their burdens, and know their troubles," the couple felt that Weil not only failed to recognize who they were, but also patronized them. Ultimately, the Bellevilles asked the friend who had introduced them to Weil to ask her to stop her visits. "My husband and I," Mme. Belleville confessed, "believed that so much learning had made the poor girl lose her wits."[44]

⁂

In the search for the origins of the modern intellectual, some historians reach back to the mid-eighteenth century and Voltaire's brave and brilliant defense of religious toleration during the Calas Affair, while others point to the late nineteenth century and the Dreyfus Affair. The earlier affair starred Jean Calas, a Protestant who was falsely accused, tortured, and executed by Catholic authorities for the murder of his son; the later affair revolved around Alfred Dreyfus, a military officer whose Jewish faith led him to be falsely accused and imprisoned for life for the crime of treason. While a number of public figures, such as Charles Maurras and Maurice Barrès, insisted on the Jewish officer's guilt, the role of intellectual was defined by those writers and academics who rallied to Dreyfus's defense because they were committed to the rational and secular values of the French Republic. They managed to parlay their prominence in specific fields, from the arts to the sciences, to pronounce publicly, through newspapers and pamphlets, on political and moral issues of universal import. Émile Zola, Jean Jaurès, and Anatole France, a few of the eminent public figures who led the Dreyfusard cause, embodied the "engaged intellectual"—a tautology of sorts since an intellectual, by definition, had to be fully engaged with the great debates that would determine the future of the republic.

At times, Dreyfusards dueled with anti-Dreyfusards; other times, street battles erupted between the two sides. Mostly, though, these intellectuals wielded pens, not swords or pistols. Yet their defense of Truth and Justice—words they themselves often capitalized—was as abstract as it was ardent. The intellectuals' devotion to the revolutionary values of liberty, equality, and fraternity led them to support the cause of the working class, but their bourgeois background blinded them to *la vie quotidienne*, the daily life, of these struggling men and women. What Weil drily observed about Marxist theorists— that most of them had never lived the lives of those they ostensibly defended—applied to nearly all intellectuals. Weil's understanding of engagement instead veers off in a radically different direction. We must, she reminded herself, get to the very roots of our ideas and ideals. Weil held this conviction to the end of her life, writing in her last work, *The Need for Roots*, that the phrase "love of truth" is misleading since truth is not an object. "A truth is always a truth with reference to something. Truth is the radiant manifestation of reality."[45]

Inevitably, Weil's repeated attempts to transform herself from an urban intellectual into a manual laborer raised the eyebrows of those who, unlike her, had no choice but to work in fields or factories. Weil acted like an ethnologist who desperately wished to go native. As Lecarpentier reminded Weil, she was "the daughter of rich people" and had no need to work on his boat. "That's my misfortune [*mon malheur*]," Weil replied. "I wish that my parents had been poor."[46] How odd that Weil, for whom *le malheur* carried such dire import, used the word to describe a situation that few others—certainly not the stunned Lecarpentier—would consider an instance of affliction. Yet, this was not—or not only—a youthful and romantic expression of rebellion against one's social class; instead, it marked a philosophical constant in Weil's thought. She considered Lecarpentier's work more authentic and more human because, unlike the mechanical labor of an assembly-line worker, it did not alienate him *from* the world. Instead, it was work that, thanks to the play of experience, skill, and applied intelligence, fully meshed *with* the world. No doubt recalling her own experience on the trawler, Weil noted that "a fisherman battling against wind and waves in his little boat, although he suffers from cold, fatigue, lack of leisure and even of sleep . . . has a more enviable lot than the manual worker on a production line, who is nevertheless better off as regards nearly all these matters."[47]

This was not mere Marxist dogma. For Hannah Arendt, the work in which Weil analyzed these issues, *La Condition ouvrière*, was "the only book in the huge literature on the labor question which deals with the problem without prejudice and sentimentality."[48] In fact, Arendt's own distinction between labor and work builds upon Weil's insights. The laborer, Arendt argues, "leaves nothing behind," and the result of his effort "is almost as quickly consumed as the effort is spent." But as we are reminded by Weil's own efforts to make ends meet, this effort, though futile, "is born of a great urgency and motivated by a more powerful drive than anything else, because life itself depends on it."[49] Work, in contrast, is the business of, well, one's hands: when they engage the world, hands are the extension of one's thoughts. Rather than being acted upon by the world, which is the lot of the laborer, the skilled worker shapes, with thought and deliberation, the material she finds in the world—an insight that also applies to the intellectual who fully engages with the world.

⁎

There is one quality, Weil believed, that we bring to the world that no other creature can: thought. "Man has nothing essentially individual about him, nothing which is absolutely his own apart from the faculty of thinking, and this society on which he is in close dependence every minute of his existence depends in turn a little on him from the moment his thinking is necessary to it."[50] Only through sustained thought, or attention, to the world and others can we locate the sources of oppression and how they ripple across our lives. But if thought does not lead to action, there is no need to have bothered thinking in the first place. In her tweak of Descartes's *cogito ergo sum*, Weil anticipates the postwar existentialist claim that our existence is established by our actions.

This conviction underscores her complex stance on violence. In this regard, like so many others, Weil was deeply impressed by the example set by Alain. Despite his advanced age (he was forty-six) and pacifist convictions, Alain had enlisted in the army once war was declared in 1914. "It seemed," he explained, "dishonorable to remain in an armchair while others are in danger."[51] Weil adopted this same stance, one not so much contradictory as consistent with her unflinching lucidity with regard to changing events and the responses they required. For the first half of the 1930s, Weil remained a steadfast pacifist. While a student at the ENS, she collared students and teachers—much to the annoyance of Célestin Bouglé—to sign a petition, published in the pacifist newspaper *La Volonté de paix*, to eliminate the military draft that enrolled graduating students into the army as officers. This gesture was especially striking when not even the most devout of Christians, Sartre later noted, "would have dared to say that one should reject violence. We thought above all of limiting it, channeling it."[52] Expanding her activities, Weil spearheaded a pacifist motion in 1929 at a meeting of the Ligue des Droits de l'Homme—the organization heaved into existence by the Dreyfus Affair—which called for universal disarmament.[53]

Weil's pacifism remained unqualified even after a month's stay in Berlin during the summer of 1932. In a long letter to her parents, who were understandably distressed that their daughter had gone to Germany at the very moment Adolf Hitler seemed on the verge of taking power, Weil described a grim cityscape of malnourished children, unemployed youths, and embattled workers. What better soil for the spread of the Nazi ideology, Weil observed, which is "astonishingly contagious, reaching inside even the Communist Party."[54] Yet even after her return, Weil refused to see war as a legitimate response to Nazism. Over the next five years, as Hitler made his geopolitical and ideological ambitions all too clear, from his invasion of the Rhineland to his threat to invade Czechoslovakia, Weil insisted war was not the answer. Rather than hastening the liberation of workers, it would enslave them to a different, and more murderous, form of technology—the instruments of modern war. This, she declared in an article titled "Reflections on War," was the "most radical form of oppression."[55] For this reason, a nation preparing for war "renders illusory all hope for liberation and protects us from nothing. Armaments races always lead to massacre."[56]

As a result, the Munich Accords were supported, but not embraced, by Weil. While the French government had a "thousand reasons" to come to terms with Hitler, Weil knew they could not conceal the ugly reality agreed upon at Munich. As for the advocates of appeasement who mocked the so-called warmongers, Weil expressed nothing but scorn. While she defended the agreement, she had no illusion as to its geopolitical and moral implications. Not only would it do nothing more than delay war, it also multiplied the effects of humiliation. With the Munich Accords, she wrote, "our humiliation is deeper than mere attachment to national pride. Each of us has felt in our very core what is the essence of humiliation: the degradation of thought by the sheer power of facts."[57]

Of course, pacifism is not the same as passivism. From antiquity to the present day, pacifists have been activists, making their case for peaceful change through various forms of nonviolent direct action. Whether by withholding sex, as with the Spartan and Athenian women in Aristophanes's comedy *Lysistrata*; withholding taxes, in the case of Henry David Thoreau; or withholding consent, in the instances of Mahatma Gandhi and Martin Luther King, Jr., pacifists have put their principles and persons on the line. This was the case with Weil. From marching with striking workers to mobilizing her fellow students, she repeatedly went to war on behalf of peace, never losing sight of the fundamental nature of her struggle, one that required action as well as analysis. "The struggle of those who obey against those command, when the mode of commanding entails destroying the human dignity of those underneath, is the most legitimate, most motivated, most genuine action that exists. There has always been this struggle, because those who command always tend, whether they realize it or not, to trample underfoot the human dignity of those below them."[58]

But as her enlistment in the Durruti Column reminds us, Weil was not an absolute pacifist. No doubt inspired by the example of Alain, she could not remain on the home front while a war raged over the future of republican Spain. Come March 1939, however, with the German invasion of the remaining tatters of an independent Czechoslovakia, Weil underwent a deeper change. In her notebooks, she records her realization—in retrospect, one that seems belated—that "non-violence is good only if it's effective." A decade later, Gandhi had the great fortune of employing his strategy of nonviolent resistance against a liberal and democratic Great Britain. A similar strategy aimed at Nazi Germany would be worse than futile, even though it did not prevent Gandhi from believing that European Jewry should practice such resistance against Hitler. Weil had taken the full measure of Nazism, and concluded that war was the only response. If for several generations, she warned, Europe was "subjected to such blind tyranny, one could not rescue what would be lost to humanity. For, contrary to what is often believed, force does destroy spiritual values and can abolish all traces of them."[59]

Come September, when France declared war on Germany following Hitler's invasion of Poland, Weil had no illusions about the effort this entailed, or its chances for success. Yet her pessimism did not entail defeatism, as was the case with so many of her former pacifist allies. In a bitter call to battle, she announced: "We must first of all have clear consciences. Do not think that we will win because we are less brutal, violent and inhuman than our enemy. Brutality, violence and inhumanity have great stature, one that textbooks hide from students and that adults try not to see, but a standing that we nevertheless acknowledge." If war was an all-or-nothing proposition, it contained fine print that bore careful reading: justice is not fated to prevail, she warned, just as goodness alone will not carry the day. Those who believed the angels were on their side posed as great a danger to France as did those wearing skulls on their uniforms. Weil warns that war is not for the fainthearted who act less brutally, violently, or inhumanely than the Nazis. Such an approach, if inspired by doubt or dithering, guarantees defeat. Instead, the critical alloy to such a successful strategy is moral rigor: "Anyone unable to be as brutal, violent and inhuman as someone else, but who also does not practice the opposing virtues, falls short of that person in inner strength and stature, and will not triumph in a confrontation."[60]

Committed to resisting Hitler, even if it meant taking up arms, Weil attacked her onetime pacifist comrades, declaring that their actions betray "a propensity to treason."[61] In this regard, she echoed Orwell's sensible observation that pacifism had become "objectively pro-fascist."[62] But she was equally harsh toward her own past, which, in her London notebooks, she damns as a "criminal error." By way of explanation, if not excuse, she wonders if her migraines were partly responsible for this mistake. Bedridden by these attacks, Weil missed several pacifist meetings, thus failing to grasp their true temper. But while debilitating headaches might serve as an excuse for many of us, not so for Weil. What truly prevented her from seeing the motivations of her fellow pacifists, she believed, "was the sin of laziness, the temptation of inertia. I desired so intensely to refrain from that sort of responsibility that I dared not consider impartially the legitimate reasons for refraining; like a seminary pupil tortured by violent carnal desires who dare not so much as look at a woman."[63] The time for nonviolent resistance, not to mention for pacifist ideals, had passed. Engagement on behalf of the good, Weil saw, meant the employment of violence.

It was no longer the case, as it was with Spain, of fighting so as not to remain on the home front. With the Nazi menace, it was the case of fighting so as to save the home front from invasion, occupation, and desolation. Or, paradoxically—even perversely—it was the case of saving the home front by bringing it to the front lines.

⁎⁎

In the late summer of 1940, while most French people wanted nothing more than a return to normalcy, Weil would have none of that. The pull of magical thinking—the belief that events would soon and favorably sort themselves out—was strong and sustained. But this pull had to be resisted: "We must keep from falling into inertia, believing that the liberation will be carried out by others. Each of us must know that one day it will be his duty to take part in it, and hold himself in readiness . . . We must think of the precious things we allowed to be lost because we did not know how to appreciate them, things that we have to regain and that we will have to preserve."[64] The key phrase is not "precious things" or "hold oneself in readiness"; instead, what makes us ready and things precious is thinking. To resist means never taking opinion for fact, conjecture for analysis, or authority for truth. It is to make the time and place to reason, just as we make the time and place to eat and sleep.

In Marseille, Weil took up the entwined activities of thinking and acting by making contact with *Cahiers du témoignage chrétien*, the underground Resistance journal launched in early 1941 by two Jesuit priests, Pierre Chaillet and Gaston Fessard, and the Protestant minister Roland de Pury. Though she did not write for the journal, Weil helped to distribute it, delivering some three hundred copies of each of the first three issues. Betrayed by the same maladroitness she showed in Spain with guns and even walking, she dropped a suitcase during one of her runs, spilling dozens of copies across the sidewalk. With remarkable sangfroid, Weil gathered and repacked the scattered papers, then continued her delivery run. One of her younger Resistance comrades, Marie-Louise Blum, was struck by Weil's personality, recalling that Weil took the time to explain to her the magnitude of their activities. Disobeying the law, Weil told Blum, is a serious affair. "One has to think it over a long time before taking the step, after assuring oneself that one has no other recourse, and that the cause which requires us to break the law is truly that of justice and truth . . . This is a necessary evil, but we should never forget that it is an evil."[65]

And it was an evil that carried enormous risks, exemplified by the arrest and deportation of a fellow delivery person. Weil was herself hauled twice to the police station for questioning. Yet the interrogations left the police more bothered than Weil, who showed the same calm with which she collected the spilled and fluttering copies of *Témoignage chrétien*. When one of her interrogators, who thought he had taken the measure of the frail and bespectacled woman, called her a "*salope* [bitch]" and threatened to toss her into a cell filled with prostitutes, Weil replied she would be glad to make their acquaintance. Shortly after, when she was released and sent home with a warning, the sense of relief at the station must have been palpable.[66]

⁂

In early 1943, Jean Cavaillès traveled to London in order to meet Charles de Gaulle. A fellow student of Weil's at the ENS, the precocious Cavaillès had been named professor of logic at the University of Strasbourg, where he specialized in the rarefied field of the philosophy of mathematics. Serving as a military officer in 1940, he earned two citations for bravery before he was taken prisoner by the Germans. Cavaillès did not remain a prisoner of war for long, though; soon escaping from his stalag, he made his way to the Unoccupied Zone. It was there that he founded, with Emmanuel d'Astier de la Vigerie, one of France's earliest Resistance networks, Libération-Sud. In late 1942, French police arrested Cavaillès, ending his two-year run of clandestine Resistance activity. But, again, not for long: Cavaillès escaped from prison and crossed the Channel the following March. After several meetings with de Gaulle, during which Cavaillès won critical material support for his group, he returned to France. Tragically, this did not last long either: arrested by German police in August, Cavaillès was packed off to the notorious prison of Fresnes, where he was repeatedly tortured. The torturers, however, never succeeded in getting the young philosopher to reveal information or names. In April 1944, they executed Cavaillès, throwing his body into a common grave, alongside a dozen other murdered *résistants*, outside the northern city of Arras. Reburied as "Inconnu no. 5 [Unknown no. 5]," Cavaillès's remains were recognized by his sister soon after liberation and transferred to the Sorbonne.

Cavaillès always denied that his acts were heroic, or that he had even chosen to act in such a way. Whenever asked why, he would always reply, "*C'est logique.*" For the logician, this was anything but a cliché. We are creatures of necessity, Cavaillès told Raymond Aron, another classmate at the ENS and a Free French recruit who would become one of the greatest intellectuals of postwar France. "The reasoning of mathematicians is necessary, the stages to mathematical theories are necessary, and the struggle we are now leading is necessary." As his fellow philosopher and *résistant* Georges Canguilhem explained, moral action is the necessary result of rigorous thought. Joining the Resistance, for Cavaillès, no more entailed a moral choice than did the solution to a mathematical problem.[67] Armed with a logic and ethic as imperious as that of his favorite thinker,

Benedict Spinoza, Cavaillès cut an imposing and inspiring figure among his colleagues.

Predictably, Cavaillès was sympathetic, but skeptical, when Weil, accompanied by Maurice Schumann, met with him during his stay in London to again plead her case to be sent to France. Though he did not discourage Weil during the meeting, Cavaillès spoke candidly to Schumann afterward. Never send Weil to France, he urged Schumann. Not only was she unfit to carry out the duties of a clandestine agent, Cavaillès insisted, but it was also the duty of everyone to serve where they were assigned. He agreed that Weil was "a case of exceptional nobility," but concluded "there is no place any longer for such cases."[68]

✳

A tragic argument for such a case was nevertheless staged in February 1944 when Jean Anouilh's *Antigone* opened at the Théâtre de l'Atelier in Paris. The young playwright, who had a weakness for Greek tragedies—*Eurydice*, his adaptation of the story of Orpheus and Eurydice, had been staged at the same theater in 1941—now used Sophocles's play to frame the nature of the German occupation of France. In the original story, the heroine Antigone ignores the order of her uncle Creon—who became king of Thebes following a bloody civil war—to leave the body of her brother (and Creon's nephew) Polynices unburied as punishment for having led a foreign army against the city. Unwavering in her insistence that divine laws trump civil laws, Antigone covers her brother's body with earth. Upon discovering his niece's act of disobedience, Creon—who insists, perhaps sincerely, that he is acting for the good of the city—condemns Antigone to death. His command in turn sparks the suicides of his own son and wife, leaving a shattered Creon to reflect on what he has done.

Two and a half millennia later, Anouilh's adaptation left his audience to reflect on what they had or had *not* done during the four years of German occupation. The Chorus's portrayal of the guards who arrest Antigone could just as easily have served as the job description of the French police: "Eternally innocent, no matter what crimes are committed; eternally indifferent, for nothing that happens matters to them." Similarly, Creon's justifications anticipate those of Philippe Pétain, the collaborationist leader of Vichy France who gave France, as he announced, "the gift of his person" as the country was collapsing in 1940: "There had to be one man who said yes. Was it a time, do you think, for playing with words like yes and no? Was it a time for a man to be weighing the pros and cons, wondering if he wasn't going to pay too dearly later on?" As for Antigone, she now seemed to channel the ethos of the French Resistance: "I can say no to anything I think vile, and I don't have to count the cost." Putting an end to Creon's attempt to strike a deal, she declares: "I will not be moderate."[69]

The audience and critics were divided over the play. The Vichy authorities rallied to Creon's dedication to the city, while their opponents were galvanized by Antigone's words and deeds. Since Weil died a year before Anouilh's play opened in Paris, it is impossible to know how she would have reacted, especially to Anouilh's portrait of Antigone. Coincidentally, in the months leading up to her death, Weil frequently referred to herself as Antigone in letters she wrote to her parents. This was, in fact, one of the monikers her family had given Weil when, even as a child, she had revealed her immoderate attachment to acting on her convictions.

For the rest of her life, Weil seemed determined to equal or exceed Antigone's devotion to duty and truth—for better and worse. Like Sophocles's heroine, Weil insisted on holding fast to her ideals, no matter the cost to herself or others. One instance, small but significant, took place when Weil was at the ENS. One of her friends, Camille Marcoux, in a presentation she gave on the political theorist Pierre-Joseph Proudhon, referred to the work of Weil's antagonist, Célestin Bouglé. Outraged by what she considered an intellectual and personal faux pas, Weil lambasted Marcoux after the class, announcing that her onetime friend was "dead" to her. The estrangement, for which Weil was the sole architect, lasted two years, and their friendship never fully recovered. Marcoux later recalled that "even though I loved her, I found it difficult to overcome a sense of separation from her, as from a person who lived on another planet."[70] This incident echoes the disagreement between Antigone and her sister Ismene over her plans to bury their brother Polynices. When Ismene pleads for caution, Antigone breaks with her, lashing out: "This sort of talk will reward you with not only my own hatred but also with that of your dead brother when you, too, will die and you will want to be near him; and he'll be right to hate you then."[71]

Weil never expressed remorse over the incident, but perhaps she felt the need to justify her behavior, if only to herself. A few years later, she sketched a portrait of Antigone that bears a striking resemblance to her own character. In *Entre Nous*, the journal published for the workers in the Bourges factory, Weil wrote a short introduction to the tragic play. *Antigone* was, she declared, "the story of a human being who, all alone, without any backing, dares to be in opposition to her own country, to the laws of the country, to the head of the government and who is, naturally, soon put to death." But this is not a reason for despair or sadness—on the contrary. A Sophoclean hero is someone who, as Weil put it elsewhere, "holds on and never lets himself be corrupted by misfortune."[72] Or, perhaps, who holds on and never lets herself remain attached to those who fall short of such austere expectations.

The paradox is that, despite the severity shown by Antigone and Weil toward others, those same "others" represent the cause embraced by these heroines. They never abandon their conviction in the necessity and rightness of resisting the economic, political, and social forces that deny our dignity and liberty as human beings. Weil is hardly confident, much less optimistic, on the success of such resistance, but that is as it should be: keeping one's eyes open is already a signal accomplishment. As Weil declared, "It is true that our weakness could prevent us from defeating the force that threatens to overwhelm us. But that does not prevent us from understanding it. Nothing in the world can stop us from being lucid."[73]

This is the same tragic, yet tempering lucidity that flows through the works of Sophocles. This is all the more true as Weil reminds us that rallying to the good in times of darkness does not mean that one's goodness will remain pure or one's effort will be rewarded. Instead, Weil believed it could "lead to a cruel and hopeless fate. To participate, even from a distance, in the unfolding of forces that drive history forward is not possible without either dirtying one's hands or condemning oneself in advance to defeat." But the near certainty of defeat cannot excuse a fall into despair. "To take refuge in indifference, or inside an ivory tower," Weil insisted, "is only possible through willed blindness."[74] She would no doubt have cheered Orwell's position on the morality of war: "We have become too civilized to grasp the obvious. For the truth is very simple. To survive you often have to fight, and to fight you have to dirty yourself. War is evil, and it is often the lesser evil. Those who take the sword perish by the sword, and those who don't take the sword perish by smelly diseases."[75]

✻

Perhaps the most feared disease, the plague, is the antagonist in Albert Camus's celebrated postwar novel. Issued in 1947, *The Plague* was based, in part, on the young French Algerian's own experiences during the occupation. By then the author of two critically acclaimed works—*The Stranger* and *The Myth of Sisyphus*—Camus was also the editor of one of the most important underground papers, *Combat*. Thanks to this prominence, he had become one of the great voices of the Resistance and of existentialism—despite his repeated efforts to deny the importance of his role in the first and his identification with the second.

By the time of the liberation of France, Camus's prestigious publisher, Gallimard, had made him one of its editors. Intent on finding new voices that could serve as political and philosophical guides for a perplexed nation, Camus began a series he called "Espoir [Hope]." While the name proved ironic—the series soon petered out—Camus had no regrets: during his brief tenure as editor he assumed responsibility for Weil's unpublished manuscripts. By the early 1950s, he had edited and published several of Weil's works, ranging from *La Source grecque* and *La Connaissance surnaturelle* to *L'Enracinement*. The encounter with Weil left an enduring mark on Camus's thought and writings. He grew close to Weil's parents, remaining in touch with them even after he stepped down as an editor. When he received the news that he had won the Nobel Prize for Literature, he took refuge at their apartment to collect his thoughts.[76] When he went to Stockholm to receive the prize in 1957, Camus was asked with which writers he felt closest. He cited just two names: the poet and close friend René Char and Simone Weil. Weil was dead, he noted, but that was not a barrier between friends.

This was not a glib observation. While Weil clearly influenced Camus's later works, it is equally clear that his earlier works already dovetailed with Weil's concerns. This is particularly striking in *The Plague*. When Camus completed the manuscript in late 1946, glumly predicting that this "complete failure will teach me modesty," he had not yet read Weil. Yet the novel's themes parallel, at times uncannily, elements in Weil's work. The plot of the novel is simple: sometime in the 1940s, the plague settles upon Oran, a city in then French Algeria. Oran's feckless political leadership refuses to name the threat for what it is, noting that the local officials could not say for certain if the plague was, indeed, the plague. Maddened by these hesitations, the book's protagonist, Doctor Rieux, exclaims: "It doesn't matter to me how you phrase it. My point is that we should not act as if there were no likelihood that half the population would be wiped out; for then it would be."[77]

Finally, when the climbing daily body count can no longer be ignored, officials close the entire city. Most of Oran's residents, who had thought the plague could never happen in their lifetime, passively submit to their lot. But a small group of individuals instead join forces to resist the plague, forming sanitary squads that care for the ill and bury the dead. At first, their motivation isn't clear. These men—a laconic doctor, an investigative journalist, a petty official, and a mysterious traveler— seem to share nothing other than being in the wrong place at the wrong time. Yet we soon discover that they also share what we might call Weil's ethic of resistance. The traveler, Jean Tarrou, expresses this code when he tells Rieux about a childhood experience, accompanying his father, a state prosecutor, to work. Watching his father argue for the death penalty, Tarrou was shocked by the contrast between the man of flesh and blood sitting in the dock and the euphemisms filling his father's closing argument.

Forever changed by the experience, Tarrou tells Rieux that we must keep an unending watch on our own selves and our words. The good man is "the man who has the fewest lapses of attention." What this comes down to, Tarrou concludes, is seeing and speaking clearly: "All of our troubles spring from our failure to use plain, clear-cut language." It is as if Rieux and Tarrou are channeling Weil's own insistence on the ethics of getting words right: "To clarify thought, to discredit intrinsically meaningless words, and to define the use of others by precise analysis—to do this, strange though it may appear, might be a way of saving human lives."[78] It is only by getting the words right—describing the world as it is—that one can act rightly and resist on behalf of others and oneself. Totalitarianism—for which the plague stands as the allegorical representation—gets words wrong. It uses them to describe a world that isn't, and thus creates a world that should never be. It comes to power through the harrowing of terror and maintains itself through the hollowing of language. This was Camus's reason for joining the French Resistance against the Nazi occupation. We were fighting, he declared, "for that fine distinction between the true and the false."

But to what end? By the time the sanitary squads help defeat the plague, Tarrou has become one of its victims. It was Tarrou, moreover, who had earlier reminded Rieux that his efforts to save his patients will never be lasting. The doctor's reply—"Yes, but it is no reason for giving up the struggle"—at first sounds pat. But instead, it sounds the depths of human purposefulness: the demand, in the face of political or ideological absurdity, for justice and dignity. In *The Rebel*, his philosophical companion to *The Plague*, Camus insists on a key element to our resistance against absurdity: "to insist on plain language so as not to increase universal falsehood."[79] Equally important, he warns that those who resist must never become those who repress, and that defending one's own dignity must never deny the dignity of others.

While struggling to finish *The Rebel*, Camus read and reread Weil's work. In his distinction between rebellion and revolution,

Camus's debt to his dead friend is especially deep. The rebel denies those who oppress and treat her as less than human, but also denies the temptation to dehumanize and mistreat that same oppressor. "It is for the sake of everyone in the world that the slave asserts himself when he comes to the conclusion that a command has infringed on something which does not belong to him alone, but which is the common ground where all men—even the man who insults and oppresses—have a natural community."[80] This is a clear echo of Weil's claim that the "struggle of those who obey against those who command, when the mode of commanding entails destroying the human dignity of those underneath, is the most legitimate, most motivated, most genuine action that exists."[81]

Moreover, Camus's concept of rebellion reflects Weil's claim for resistance: both are centered on the necessity of moderation. In her *Reflections*, Weil declared that lucidity with oneself as well as others "does away with insatiable desires and vain fears; from this and not from anything else proceed moderation and courage, virtues without which life is nothing but a disgraceful frenzy."[82] A half-dozen years later, in the *Iliad* essay, she has not relinquished her belief in the need for limits. The Western world, she wrote, no longer even has a word to "express it in any of its languages: conceptions of limit, measure, equilibrium which ought to determine the conduct of life are, in the West, restricted to a servile function in the language of technics."[83] Similarly, Camus insisted that, as the ancient Greeks remind us, measure is immeasurably important. The lesson of ancient tragedy, he wrote, is that "limit must not be transgressed . . . To make a mistake about this limit, to try to destroy the balance, is to perish."[84] Indeed, both are infatuated by the source for these ideas—ancient Greece—just as both were repelled by what they considered its antithesis, ancient Rome. But the ties that bind Camus and Weil to ancient Greece, as well as to one another, come undone when it comes to the ultimate source of these ideas and ideals. Camus refused to look beyond our world, while Weil, transfixed between the Good and God, could not help but look beyond our world.

CHAPTER FOUR

Finding Roots

You know what I am? I'm a
nationalist. OK? I'm a nationalist.

DONALD TRUMP

Without history there can be no sense of patriotism.
We have only to look at the United States to see what it is
to have a people deprived of the time-dimension.

SIMONE WEIL

Stout was not among the many things Weil loved about England. When asked about the dark beer by her parents, she explained that she could not drink a glass without eating something with it. Yet there was no food to be had in a pub, where one normally drinks such brews. But there was something else to be had in pubs—namely, an introduction to the English character. "Did I ever tell you," Weil wrote, "that a pub and a bistro, side by side, would show more eloquently than many big volumes the difference between the two peoples—their history, their temperament, and the way the social question presents itself for each of them?"[1]

Pubs, Weil observes, are divided by a partition that runs from the counter to the back wall. On one side is the "public bar," furnished with a couple of benches and a dartboard. Standing in groups, beer in hand, the patrons busily converse; they are, Weil notes, "very happy." This is not the case, however, on the other side of the partition, called the "saloon." The same drinks are served there, but it is furnished with small tables and chairs. The patrons on this side of the partition seem better off, Weil thought, but they also "seem less happy." There is, Weil thought, "a symbol here."[2]

Apart from noting that the denizens of the public bar "have a great deal of dignity," Weil does not explain what, exactly, the pub symbolizes. Perhaps it was because by June 1943, when she wrote this letter, she no longer had the strength or attention to develop her observation. By then, Weil had been a patient at Middlesex Hospital for a month, admitted when a colleague, surprised not to see Weil at her desk, passed by her rented room and found her unconscious on the floor. When the hospital staff diagnosed tuberculosis, they faced an odd complication: although there was food (if not stout) to be had, Weil refused to eat. As she had earlier warned Maurice Schumann, "I cannot eat the bread of the English without taking part in their war effort."[3]

Especially if that bread was served in a glass. Even before her collapse, Weil rarely visited pubs. She makes little mention of them elsewhere in her letters, and during the four short months she lived in London, she spent most of her time either at the Free French offices at Hill Street or in her rented room in Holland Park. When she did walk around London, Weil preferred Hyde Park and its public speakers, a scene that reminded her of the agora in ancient Athens, to the public houses.[4]

But the symbolic attraction of the pub, at least for Weil, is not difficult to grasp. Like the ingredients that make stout (the barley and oats rooted in the English countryside), the ingredients that make pubs (the customs and practices of the English people) are rooted in what, for want of a better phrase, we must call the "English way of life." Upon seeing a performance of *Twelfth Night*, Weil insisted there was "no break in continuity between Shakespeare's drinking scenes and the atmosphere of London pubs today."[5] Had she instead seen a performance of *Henry V*, she might well have similarly declared that there was no break in continuity between Henry's Saint Crispin Day's speech and England's resilience in the face of the German onslaught.

The persistence of a people is tied to the persistence of their culture—a community's deeply engrained way of life, which bends but is not broken as it carries across generations. It is perhaps not a coincidence that Weil—an exile from the country she desperately wished to return to—explored this phenomenon in England during the final months of her life. Nor, perhaps, is it a coincidence that, in May, she told her parents. "I have done another 'magnum opus,' or rather I am doing one, because it is not finished yet." But it was, Weil added, a work that would be mostly ignored: "Naturally, I don't think there is the slightest reason to suggest that what I am writing will have any effect. But as you can guess, that doesn't stop me from writing."[6] Her parents would have guessed that, of course. What they did not guess, however, was that by the time their daughter wrote this letter, she had already spent a month in the hospital. Weil did not name this magnum opus, but she undoubtedly meant her final work, *L'Enracinement*, or *The Need for Roots*.

☆

For the better part of the twentieth century, French intellectuals had a weakness for roots. There was, in particular, a rage for roots among conservative and extreme right-wing thinkers. As early as the last decades of the nineteenth century, they were inventing new recipes for *les racines*. The founder of the extreme right-wing group Action Française, Charles Maurras, first won notoriety as a regionalist who sought to defend his native Provençal culture from the ravages of republican institutions founded on abstract and ostensibly universal principles. Maurras famously struck the contrast between *le pays réel*—

regions like Provence or Brittany whose soils nurture distinct and different peoples—and *le pays légal*, the fictitious nation of France heaved into existence by a distant and disconnected republican state.

His fellow radical conservative, the writer Maurice Barrès, was an indefatigable journalist and influential politician. He was also a best-selling novelist, most famous for his 1897 pot-boiler *Les Déracinés* (The Uprooted). In this novel, the first volume in his trilogy *Le Roman de l'énergie national* (The Novel of National Energy), Barrès traces the trajectories of several provincial youths from his native Lorraine. Uprooting themselves from their natal soil and moving to Paris to attend university, they become easy prey for the foreign and abstract philosophy of Immanuel Kant. But these French twenty-somethings, once they are exposed to the *Critique of Pure Reason*, can no more flourish than could Gamay grapevines rooted in Parisian asphalt. The novel climaxes in bloodstained madness when two of the students, whose "Lorraine souls" have been deformed by their Kantian professor, murder a woman. The moral is clear: having quit their native earth to become worldly, these youths have instead withered.

Both Maurras and Barrès portrayed the French nation in irrational terms, as the product of untold generations tied to the land and one another. For Barrès, France was defined by *la terre et les morts*—by the people who worked and were buried in the same soil. As for Maurras, though he was not a practicing Catholic, he nevertheless latched onto the Church as the foundation for a France based on hierarchy and order. He asserted that France was the product of throne and altar, the monarchy and the Catholic Church, sacred institutions that had shaped France for nearly a millennium before the profane rupture of 1789. While the two thinkers differed in several important respects, both saw the republic as a historical mistake that needed correction. They also both shared a robust anti-Semitism, which made no room for Jews in the French nation. Maurras's Action Française was hatched in the ideological incubator of the Dreyfus Affair, while Barrès excluded Jews from his definition of the French nation. "Jews have no *patrie* in the sense we ascribe to that word. For us, the *patrie* is the soil of the ancestors, the earth of our dead. For them, it is wherever they find their greater interest."[7]

Both thinkers represented an ideological current that the historian Zeev Sternhell has labeled "the revolutionary right."[8] This is not the sort of company that Weil kept. She was as repelled by Barrès's romantic irrationalism as she was by Maurras's pragmatic Catholicism, not to mention by the street violence of his movement. As David McClellan rightly notes, Weil did not "share Barrès's worship of the earth and the dead and her conception of hierarchy and order were far from those of Maurras."[9] But what she did share was a dim view of the prerogatives of the state (whether in capitalist or communist guise) to shape the lives of citizens, of intellectuals who prattle in abstractions and pretend to speak for the people without knowing anything about them, and of the false and fatal allure of revolution. These were all symptomatic of what she identified as Europe's greatest threat: *déracinement*, "uprootedness."

Wherever Weil looked, she saw the debris and despair caused by uprootedness. It was a preexisting condition, she believed, that explained the sudden defeat of France in 1940: "A tree whose roots are almost entirely eaten away falls at the first blow."[10] By 1943, it was not only an affliction she and her parents suffered, but one that had become the default position of millions of other Europeans. Occurring whenever there is military conquest, rootlessness reaches "its most acute stage when there are deportations on a massive scale, as in Europe under the German occupation."[11] But this violent action is not limited to the deportation of peoples; it also applies to the "brutal suppression of all local traditions," including what French colonial authorities, Weil believed, were doing in the colonies. While the gravity of such activities is clear, less clear is what Weil would have concluded had she known that the Nazi deportations of Jews were leading not just to the suppression of their traditions, but to their very eradication as a people.

Nevertheless, Weil's notion of uprooting captures one of modernity's defining characteristics: the fact and feeling of homelessness. For Weil, the act of uprooting is not just physical, but also social and psychological; one can be uprooted without ever having moved or having been moved. What Thomas Carlyle called the "cash nexus"—the transformation of all human relationships into monetary transactions—pollutes our traditional and nurturing places. "Money destroys human roots wherever it is able to penetrate," Weil writes, "and manages to outweigh all other motives, because the effort it demands of the mind is so very much less. Nothing is *so* clear and *so* simple as a row of numbers."[12] The rationalization and industrialization of the workplace grinds into bits the moral roots of countless workers. "Although they have remained geographically stationary, they have been morally uprooted, banished and then reinstated, as it were on sufferance, in the form of industrial brawn."[13] The bonds that once existed among artisans—the traditions and travels of masters and journeymen that tied them to the past and future—had been snapped. As a result, Weil writes, "each thing is looked upon as an end in itself." The consequences are a catastrophe to which we have grown accustomed, being taught to embrace ends, not means; to see others as objects, not subjects; and to accept what Weil calls idolatry, and forget the integrity that once defined our relationship to work and ourselves.[14]

Between her first magnum opus—her own wry description of her *Reflections concerning the Causes of Liberty and Social*

Oppression—and her second one, Weil traveled a great distance, moving beyond a critique of society that is materialist and, in her peculiar way, Marxist. Instead, Weil is now offering a moral, political, and, yes, spiritual perspective, one that manages to be both more radical and more conservative than her previous position. Finding Marx's notion of alienation too dry and narrow, Weil now points to a deeper and more elusive trait. By rootedness, she anticipates Robert Putnam's notion of social capital. In his landmark study *Bowling Alone*, Putnam marshaled vast amounts of statistical evidence to make manifest the decay of American civic institutions that many observers had already intuited. With the decline in civic associations, there has been a concomitant decline in civic values, a state of affairs that has led to a crippling deficit of social capital. Unable to fall back on the traditional organizations or institutions that once formed and informed our lives, we now mostly go bowling alone.

Or, in the case of interwar France, playing *pétanque* alone. Weil had already witnessed the atomization and anomie bred in the factories, and the sense of having become forgotten or invisible on the farms. The widespread sense of disconnection that Putnam explores had already been captured by Weil, just as the causes he cites for this disconnection resemble those Weil lists and glosses. Foreign invasion is not the only driver of the uprooting of a people. While less immediate and dramatic in its impact, industrialization, and the accompanying rationalization of work, also ripped men and women from their habitual places. Reduced to cogs in a machine, whether as machine workers at Alsthom or warehouse workers at Amazon, the "majority of working men," Weil asserts, "have experienced the sensation of no longer existing, accompanied by a sort of inner vertigo, such as intellectuals or bourgeois, even in their greatest sufferings, have very rarely had the opportunity of knowing."[15]

Similarly, both Putnam and Weil also finger mass media as

principal culprits of this lamentable state of affairs. While Putnam concludes that television is the "single most consistent predictor" of civic decay (the internet and social media were still in their infancy when *Bowling Alone* appeared in 2000), Weil's observation of radio, movies, and magazines is even more harsh. Uprooting is enabled, in part, "by the setting up of the wireless and cinemas in the villages, and by the sale of newspapers like *Confidences* and *Marie-Claire* [women's weeklies] compared with which cocaine is a harmless product."[16]

Ultimately, *The Need for Roots* reflects Weil's persistent attachment to principles that were conservative, though not at all Barrèsian or Maurrasian. Instead, they were distinctly English. During the months she spent in England before her death, Weil cited Shakespeare and Dickens in her letters, and encouraged her mother to read A. E. Housman's *A Shropshire Lad*.[17] Yet Weil seems not to have read another English writer—more accurately, an Anglo-Irishman who settled in England—with whom she nevertheless had much in common: Edmund Burke. Just as Burke's strain of what we can call, without irony, compassionate conservatism drove his fellow Tories mad, Weil's conception of compassionate patriotism found few friends on the French left. "To make us love our country," Burke observed, "our country must be lovely." Similarly, Weil insisted that the state, which had helped to uproot the French, was incapable of being loved: "The State is a cold concern which cannot inspire love, but itself kills, suppresses everything that might be loved."[18] Just as Burke warned against the fatal presumptions of the French revolutionaries, Weil was equally harsh with contemporaries who clamored for a revolution. Burke had asked, why bother "discussing a man's abstract right to food or medicine" when the point is to find a "method of procuring and administering them"—a method that farmers and physicians, not metaphysicians, could best suggest.

Similarly, Weil excoriated the left's romance with revolution, declaring that it is a "word for which you kill, for which you die, for which you send the laboring masses to their death, but which does not possess any content."[19] Just as Burke dismissed the revolution's call for equality ("Those who attempt to level never equalize"), Weil saw all too clearly that the revolution in Russia led to a new and even more oppressive hierarchy. Although the two thinkers wildly diverged on matters ranging from the place of political parties—Burke insisted on their necessity, while Weil insisted on their noxiousness—to the role of religious faith, they converged on the primacy of rootedness. Though the word does not appear, at least in the sense used by Weil, in Burke's *Reflections on the Revolution in France*, it nevertheless undergirds his thought. "To be attached to the subdivision, to love the little platoon we belong to in society," he declares, "is the first link in the series by which we proceed towards our love of country and to mankind." But these roots of attachment, which sprout and grow in a common soil, burrow not just across space, but across time, forming "a partnership not only between those who are living, but between those who are dead and those who are to be born." For both thinkers, a partnership entails a sense of obligation and call to duty, not just to the past but also to the present, not just to one's ancestors but also to one's contemporaries. When Weil declares that "all human beings are bound by identical obligations, although they are performed in different ways according to particular circumstances," it is as if she is channeling Burke. It is not an accident that in his final book on conservatism, the late English philosopher Roger Scruton places both Burke and Weil in what he calls the "great tradition."[20]

✲

In her essay on the *Iliad*, Weil introduces roots only to pull them up. Agamemnon, having been shamed by Achilles, butchers his way through the ranks of the Trojans, Homer comparing his blood-soaked rampage to a "fire consuming dry manzanita when the winds rise up / And the scrub forest is burned to its roots."[21] But in Weil's account of the poem, Odysseus makes little more than a cameo appearance. Apart from citing his early speech urging the Achaeans not to quit their struggle before they take Troy—the city for which "we have suffered so much"—Weil ignores the "much-enduring and brilliant" Greek warrior. In fact, not only does she wave off Odysseus, she is equally dismissive of the epic that carries his name. While the *Iliad* is "the only true epic the Occident possesses," the *Odyssey* "seems merely a good imitation, now of the *Iliad*, now of Oriental poems."[22] For Weil, the *Iliad* is the epic of force, while the *Odyssey* is a poem of farce.

As sometimes happens with Weil, her judgment of the *Odyssey* is incisive, but also invidious. It is also decidedly odd, given the role of roots in this Homeric sequel. While the prospect of uprooting is never distant in the *Iliad*, the promise of rooting is always close in the *Odyssey*. From Odysseus's first appearance in the poem, sitting on the rocks of Calypso's island, "wrenching his heart with sobs and groans and anguish / gazing out over the barren sea through blinding tears," the theme of *nostos*, the longing for a "homecoming," swells through the epic. The climax occurs in the penultimate book, when Odysseus, having returned to his native Ithaca after an absence of twenty years, meets his wife, Penelope. Uncertain whether this "strange man" is, as he insists, her husband, Penelope orders her maid to move the bridal bed from its place for this visitor's comfort. A shocked Odysseus explodes that only a god could move the bed, reminding Penelope that he had built it himself from a massive olive tree still rooted in the ground. "Does the bed, my

lady," he bellows, "still stand planted firm? / I don't know—or
has someone chopped away that olive-trunk and hauled our bedstead off?"[23]

It still held firm, of course. There are, to this very day, olive
trees on Crete that might be old enough to serve as backdrop
to a Greek bard chanting the very same epic. Yet for all their
resilience and tenacity, olive trees—for the ancient Romans,
the "first of all trees"—nevertheless present something of a paradox. They owe their longevity not to roots that dig deep, but
instead to roots that wander wide. It is thanks to a root system
that clings close to the surface that olive trees prosper in the
arid regions of the Mediterranean littoral.

There is something profound about this shallowness. What
Friedrich Nietzsche said of the ancient Greeks—they lived
well because they knew to "keep bravely to the surface"—also
applies to their beloved tree. Rootedness, Christy Wampole has
observed, "is the precondition for verticality"—another word
for "transcendence," the movement upward that, at least for
many of us, leads to reverence and perhaps even revelation.[24]
But for the olive tree, survival is not a matter of verticality, at
least when it comes to its roots. It is not anchored, like the fig
tree, by deep taproots that plunge hundreds of feet, or even,
like the grapevine, by roots that burrow dozens of feet into the
ground. Instead, a tree that reaches a height of forty feet and, in
certain cases, an age of more than two thousand years depends
on the horizontality, not verticality, of its root system. The tan-
gle of roots anchoring the tree is both extensive, radiating far
beyond the tree's canopy, and also shallow, rendering it vulnerable to natural and manmade dangers. Mere horizontality sparks
a different kind of reverence than does sheer verticality—a reverence that deepens when we recall how easy it is to uproot olive
trees. Perhaps Odysseus should not have been so shocked when
Penelope suggested that the bedstead could easily be moved.

The superficiality of this root system inspires awe, but also anxiety—so much depends on something so easily exposed. Its horizontal and vulnerable character resembles, in effect, the same qualities found at Ithaca. The olive tree from which Odysseus carved his bed stood at the very center of his *oikos*, the fundamental social unit; like the tree's roots, the reach of the *oikos* extended far beyond Odysseus's palace. As Moses Finley notes, the *oikos* was the "center around which life was organized, from which flowed not only the satisfaction of material needs, including security, but also ethical norms and values, duties, obligations and responsibilities."[25] As with any authentic community, the *oikos* is what gives its members a sense of identity and purpose.

Weil lacked this sense of place when she wrote *The Need for Roots*. Like millions of other Europeans, she had been uprooted from a place that, despite its many flaws, had been her place. In July 1942, soon after arriving in New York with her parents, Weil wrote to Maurice Schumann, describing how her separation from France had become a never healing wound. Even living under Vichy, she still had the consolation "of sharing in the country's suffering," as well as the sense that to be separated from France "would hurt me more from a distance than when I was there. And so it does; and the passing of time only makes the pain more unbearable. Moreover, I have the feeling that by leaving France I committed an act of desertion. This thought is intolerable. To leave was like tearing up my roots."[26] But Weil makes clear that roots find their sustenance in places other than the soil of rural France. For her, cities no less than villages offer a nurturing sense of place. As she explained, in English, to a British officer: "My life is of no value to me as long as Paris, my native city, is subject to German domination."[27]

Weil's open wound—the visceral sense of having been torn from France, the one place where she could flourish—is the emotional source for her last work. Yet she scorns the patriotic fictions that portray France as a pure good. Instead, it is impure and imperfect, like any other place. In a passage as autobiographical as it is analytical, she reflects upon this fact. "In defining one's native country as a certain particular vital medium, one avoids the contradictions and lies which corrode the idea of patriotism . . . It has been produced by a network of causes in which good and evil, justice and injustice have been mixed up together, and so it cannot be the best possible one. It may have arisen at the expense of some other combination richer in vital properties, and if such has been the case, it would be right to regret the fact; but past events are over and done with; the particular medium happens to be in existence, and, such as it is, deserves to be guarded like a treasure for the good it contains."[28]

Nevertheless, by the end of her life, Weil had come to see one particular evil, that of colonization, as the key to understanding what, precisely, was at stake. France was, of course, threatened by the particular brand of imperialism that drove the Germans across Europe. Moreover, as the nature of Nazism made clear, this imperialism unmade the colonizer no less than the colonized. But in a twist that could not have pleased de Gaulle, who was intent on preserving the French empire, Weil insisted that this same analysis applied to France. The imperialism that drove France to seize lands across the Mediterranean had uprooted the French as it did their so-called subject peoples, with devastating moral consequences for both the one and the other.

∗⁎

The year 1931 marked the close of Weil's studies at the ENS and the opening of the Colonial Exposition in Paris. The contempt she felt for teachers like Bouglé shifted to her fellow French and their attitude toward the colonies of France. What the Eiffel

Tower was to the 1889 exposition, the temple of Angkor Wat was to the Colonial Exposition. It was an authentic reproduction of the magnificent Cambodian temple, which French archaeologists had already begun to restore. The literally spectacular message of this reproduction was that the once flourishing civilizations now absorbed by France should welcome their beneficent overseers. As its director declared, the mission of the exposition was to place "before the eyes of its visitors an impressive summary of the results of colonization."[29]

Before she visited the exposition, Weil had read an appalling account in *Le Petit Parisien* of the French government's treatment of the inhabitants of the protectorate of Annam. This was the moment, she later recalled, when "I felt and understood the tragedy of colonization." Her "heart burdened by the misery and slavery of the Annamites, and the unpunished insolence of the whites" who ruled over them, Weil decided to tour the exposition.[30] Standing in front of the reproduction of Angkor Wat, Weil dismissed it as a monumental work of propaganda, furious at visitors who, gawping at the sight, were "stupidly indifferent to the suffering caused by the regime thus symbolized."[31]

Weil's fury raged for the rest of the decade, years during which she published a number of articles attacking French colonial policy. In part, this may have been, as Simone Pétrement suggests, because it was one issue where Weil, discouraged by the incomprehension or indifference that greeted her articles on other matters, believed she could still wield influence.[32] There was, as well, her burning sense of shame as a citizen of a republic that refused to grant its founding liberties to the peoples it ruled. "By depriving peoples of their tradition, of their past, and thus of their soul, colonization reduces them to the state of matter, but matter that is human. The populations of occupied countries are just this in the eyes of the Germans. But it cannot be denied that the majority of the colonials have the same attitude toward the natives."[33]

By 1943, Weil had come to see colonization as the root cause of the ills that afflicted the world. France was not merely occupied by the Germans; instead, it had been colonized by them. It was this act of colonization that the Resistance movements sought to end. It was thus essential that the war against Germany not obscure the brute fact of French colonization of other peoples. "The harm that Germany would have done to Europe if Britain had not prevented the German victory is the harm that colonization does, in that it uproots people. It would have deprived people of their past. The loss of the past is the descent into colonial enslavement." Determined to confront de Gaulle, for whom the colonies were essential to both national grandeur and international influence, Weil declared: "This harm which Germany tried in vain to do to us, we did to others."[34]

The tragic irony was inescapable: France's enslavement of others was done in the spirit of the liberating principles of 1789. As a result, French imperialism—so different from its British counterpart, Weil observes, which was based on nothing more elevated than commercial interests—is morally and ideologically incoherent. "Either the natives feel disrupted in their attachment to their own tradition by this foreign contribution. Or else they sincerely adopt these principles and rebel against the fact that they get no benefit from them."[35] Given the reality of French rule in the colonies, any effort to maintain the fiction of the so-called civilizing mission borders on the criminal. "We can no longer say or think that we have received from on high the mission to teach the universe how to live."[36]

As a position paper for the Free French, Weil's argument was suicidal. At the very moment de Gaulle was trying to rally the support of French colonial leaders, a member of his staff was insisting that France's role as a colonial power was untenable.

The dynamic between a totalitarian Germany and a republican France was, for Weil, identical to the dynamic between an imperial France and its imperial subjects. Just as France, along with the rest of Europe, risked material and spiritual annihilation at the hands of the Nazi overlords, so too did the colonized in Africa, Asia, and the Pacific face the same fate at the hands of their French overlords. The moral and psychological consequences of losing one's past were as great for the Polynesians or Annamites living under French rule as for the French living under German rule. For Weil, regardless of where colonization occurs, its consequences are equally destructive.

Yet Weil once again struck a balance between morality and reality, acknowledging the latter while insisting that it did not tarnish the former. Although the French past was rooted in morally indefensible actions abroad and at home, the present and future of France nevertheless needed to be defended. To have a nation, for Weil, is essential, no matter the injustices committed in its name in the past. As she later argued, this contradiction lies at the heart of the human condition. Just as soil is inevitably an admixture of healthy nutrients and potentially toxic substances, rootedness in a finite and flawed community is the basis for a moral and intellectual life that strives to overcome these limits. What better way, Weil asked, to reinforce such a life than by confronting the past? Nazi Germany, she insists, is not the sole source of French ills. The experience of the French under the German swastika should stir, not stifle our conscience about colonial peoples living under the French tricolor. Weil's conclusion is as impolitic as it is imperative: the struggle of France against the imperialism of Nazi Germany entails a similar struggle against its own imperial activities.

Ultimately, Weil traces how the fervor for nationhood in 1789 morphed into the fever for conquest. With a fearful symmetry, the rooting of the French people—the invention of this partic-

ular nation—entailed the uprooting of other peoples, especially
in Africa and Asia. She warned that we cannot invoke France's
calling in the world—a vocation self-evident even to her Free
French colleagues—"with unmixed pride unless we lie to ourselves." For this pride was enabled by a kind of magical thinking
that assumed that France, because it had managed until then
to straddle this "contradiction inherent in French patriotism,"
would continue to do so after its liberation. But nothing, she
warns, will be as it was before the war. Having alluded to the
moral stain of imperialism, Weil clearly warns her superiors
that France, once liberated, cannot reiterate its colonial policy.
Aware that this is a policy paper, in principle meant for the eyes
of Charles de Gaulle, Weil announces that a "terrible responsibility" rests with those who will govern postwar France. "For it
is nothing less than a question of refashioning the soul of the
country, and the temptation is so strong to do this by resorting
to lies or half-lies that it requires more than ordinary heroism
to remain faithful to the truth."[37]

Inevitably, Weil herself fell short of this ideal at times. Her
insistence on the truth did not immunize her from a number
of political and moral blind spots. Her persistent focus on the
crimes of French imperialism blurred the far greater crimes of
Nazism. When she asks rhetorically if it is as difficult to ignore
the "cruelties of the Germans towards the Jews or Czechs as it
is of those of the French towards the Annamites," she reveals
a shocking lack of measure. By early 1943, Weil seems to have
been willfully blind to the character and consequences of Nazi
anti-Semitism. It is astonishing that someone who had been to
Germany, where she directly encountered Nazism, persisted in
her belief that what the Germans were doing to Jews was the
equivalent of what the Germans were doing to the Czechs, not
to mention what the French had done to the Annamites. The
transformation of human beings into ashes was taking place not

in French colonies of Amman or Algeria, but in the Nazi death camps of eastern Europe.

In her attraction to absolutes, Weil also overlooks crucial details that nuance the character of French imperialism. In *The Need for Roots*, Weil cites one of the many variations of the famous line from Ernest Lavisse's late nineteenth-century history primer ("Our ancestors, the Gauls, had blond hair"), marveling at the implicit violence done to Polynesian children forced to recite it.[38] But is it possible that Weil was also blind, if only to the ability of both the colonized students and teachers to make sense, or nonsense, of such claims? When Weil was a *lycée* student in Paris, the poet Aimé Césaire was growing up in Martinique. When he and his classmates repeated this line at their school, he recalls, "the teacher laughed along with the rest of us. After all, we were all Negroes."[39] Moreover, Weil seems to assume, despite the many ways she had herself resisted the state curricula as a teacher, that all teachers in the colonies were complicit with the government's curricula. Yet, as historians of French colonialism now argue, there was often a great distance between the texts required by Paris and the use made of them by local teachers. Moreover, during the 1920s, French colonial officials themselves began to shift the focus of their policies from assimilation to association, giving greater leeway and support to local cultures.[40] Though the reasons for this shift were hardly altruistic, and though the French occupied lands not their own and ruled peoples against their will, the terms of the occupation and flexibility of these rules nevertheless varied.

Moreover, Weil was herself conflicted over how best to define the relationship of France to its colonial subjects, and how best to time the granting of full independence. On the one hand, she insisted that France's imperial subjects should, in fact, be granted their subjectivity—in other words, that they must not be treated as objects who constitute nothing more than a resource for French geopolitical ambitions. Yet, on the other hand, Weil seemed reluctant to hand them their full independence—at least if such independence was based on foreign paradigms. To make these peoples like "nations on the European model, whether democratic or not, would be no better," Weil warned. "There are already too many nations in the world." Instead, she suggested a form of "protection," a vaguely defined relationship that would grant these peoples their freedom but would some- how still tie them to "certain organized states."[41] Remarkably, despite the attention she devoted to this existential issue, Weil nevertheless seemed either unwilling or unable to acknowledge that a growing number of the very people on whose behalf she spoke were no longer interested in such ties.

⁂

Although nationalism is of recent vintage, patriotism is as ancient as the Athens of Pericles or the Gaul of Vercingetorix. Like an accordion, it is a sentiment, Weil believed, that "expands or contracts according to the degrees of similarity and common danger."[42] For centuries, she argued, there was no "definite, cir- cumscribed thing" on which this sentiment could settle and grow. With the events of 1789, patriotism became the posses- sion of the revolutionary nation in arms, but not for long. The state soon laid claim to it, reducing the word "nation," which once denoted a sovereign people, to "the sum total of peoples recognizing the authority of the same State."[43] More disturb- ingly, the history not just of the twentieth century, but of our own era as well, reveals how easily that authority can be claimed by a lone individual, "acclaimed as leader and at his side the iron-bound machine of State."[44]

Hence Weil's irritation with patriots and nationalists who posit the nation as the ultimate source of value in their lives.

Weil quite literally puts nations, and thus nationalists, in their place. "The nation is a fact, and a fact is not an absolute value."[45] Besides, there is nothing intrinsic to the nature of nationalism that leads to the invasion and occupation of other nations. Yet from the late nineteenth to the early twentieth century, the French Third Republic fused nationalism and imperialism. Weil believed that this reflex predates the very notion of the nation, not to mention nationalism. While in Marseille with her parents, Weil turned her attention to the Albigensian Crusade. As I earlier noted, this particular crusade, launched by the French crown at the turn of the thirteenth century, was aimed not at infidels in Jerusalem, but at heretics closer to home. The French monarchy invaded the *pays d'Oc*, the lands south of the Loire River, where the distinct culture, religion, and language of Occitania flourished. Over the course of two decades, the French forces proved too powerful, ravaging the lands and uprooting by terror and mass executions the religious and political classes. To the men and women of Occitania, Weil wrote, "the French were as much foreigners and barbarians as the Germans are to us."[46]

The essential nutrient for the flourishing of patriotism, as Weil sees it, is not pride, but compassion. Patriotism is fueled by sympathy, and not antipathy, for others. Such a notion will strike most of us as simply bizarre. It clashes, obviously, with the patriotism declared in "La Marseillaise," which calls for watering the soil of France with the blood of its enemies. For that matter, it clashes with our own "Star-Spangled Banner," whose third and mostly unfamiliar stanza announces that the blood of British invaders "has washed out their foul footsteps' pollution." Indeed, Weil's conception of patriotism is as bizarre as her plan to parachute unarmed nurses onto battlefields. How tempting to blurt, as did de Gaulle, that Weil's reflections on compassion are, like her proposal for airborne nurses, the ravings of a lunatic.

But are they? By 1943, Weil had forsworn the pacifism she espoused for most of her life. In fact, she now treated this earlier stance like a hair shirt, never missing the opportunity to lacerate herself for what she came to see as a grave mistake. Weil recognized the need for violence to oppose Hitler; as for Gandhi's pacifism, once again, it makes sense with an occupier like the British, but is nonsensical when applied to the Nazis. Had the French acted on Gandhi's principles, "far greater numbers would have perished, and in more frightful circumstances."[47] Besides, had she herself not sought active service as an undercover agent, lamenting her decision to have left France in 1942? When Weil writes that duty toward one's country "does not require that we should give everything always, but that we should give everything sometimes," she is making place for both compassion and force. Anticipating, perhaps influencing, Albert Camus's distinction between rebellion and revolution, Weil argues for a form of resistance that encompasses both the effort to repel the Germans as occupiers and the effort to recall Germans as fellow human beings.[48] Let no one imagine, she asserts, that compassion for one's own country "excludes war-like energy."[49]

Yet, Weil also asserts that compassion is an equal-opportunity sentiment, one that is "able, without hindrance, to cross frontiers, extend itself over all countries in misfortune, over all countries without exception; for all peoples are subjected to the wretchedness of our human condition."[50] Unlike pride in one's nation, which is incapable of export to other nations, compassion for one's own nation is, by its very nature, a universal impulse. To cultivate this sentiment is not only laudable, but also practical because it tightens the bonds of fraternity both between peoples and within a single people. For this reason, Weil insists, we must portray our country not only as beautiful and precious, but also as "imperfect [and] very frail."[51]

☆☆

Weil's own conception of the nation shares a number of traits with earlier attempts at defining the concept. Though she dismisses as "mediocre" Ernest Renan's answer to the question "What Is a Nation?" (the title of his celebrated essay, published in 1882), Weil nevertheless echoes Renan's key points. He held that two elements, one rooted in the past and the other in the present, constitute the nation. "One is the possession in common of a rich legacy of remembrances; the other is the actual consent, the will to live together, the will to continue to value the heritage which all hold in common."[52] Add "future" to the mix, and Renan's definition scarcely differs from Weil's own description of the nation: it "constitutes the supreme mission of society towards the individual human being, namely, maintaining throughout the present the links with the past and the future."[53]

An even more uncanny parallel to Weil's notion of nationalism is the latitudinarian and liberal vision of Johann Gottfried Herder. One of the eighteenth century's most original yet overlooked thinkers, Herder not only invented the term "nationalism" (*Nationalismus*), but is also widely seen as its greatest champion. Like Weil, he was repelled by the Enlightenment invocation of universal ideals derived from reason; like Weil, he was outraged by the ravages caused by the imperial spirit of French political and intellectual classes. Herder railed against the spread of the French language, labeling it a "cancer" to other cultures. In *The Need for Roots*, Weil affirms that the people of the *pays d'Oc* in the thirteenth century "were filled with an intensely patriotic feeling for what they termed their 'language'—a word which, for them, was synonymous with native land."[54] Herder likewise thought language the very essence of a people. "The very first words we stammer," he declared, "are the foundation stones of our knowing." As a result, the bleeding of French—by then the dominant language of diplomacy and philosophy, literature and love—into the lives of other peoples risked turning Europe into a vast graveyard of other languages and cultures.

Although both Herder and Weil were patriots, even nationalists, they have little in common with many of those who now claim that label. Both of these thinkers insisted that every civilization was unique and incommensurable with others; a nation's ways and wisdom, language and lore can be measured only against its own standard. The claim of incommensurability, by doing away with the existence of a single standard, renders pointless the insistence upon the greatness of one's nation. "To brag of one's country," Herder declared more than a century before Weil, "is the stupidest form of boastfulness." Asking what a nation is, Herder replies: "It is a great wild garden full of bad plants and good."[55]

The resonances between Herder's and Weil's views are remarkable. In her emphasis on rootedness as the necessary condition of a living culture, it is as if she took a leaf from Herder's writings. Comparing a culture to a particular patch of soil, she asserts: "There is one's own particular vital medium; but there are others besides. It has been produced by a network of causes in which good and evil, justice and injustice have been mixed up together, and so it cannot be the best possible one. It may have arisen at the expense of some other combination richer in vital properties, and if such has been the case, it would be right to regret the fact; but past events are over and done with; the particular medium happens to be in existence and, such as it is, deserves to be guarded like a treasure for the good it contains."[56] Since each and every nation has taken root in soil specific to its time and place, each and every one is utterly unique. As a result, no one nation can serve as a standard for another nation, nor can the leader of one nation dismiss another nation, as has President Donald Trump, as a "shithole."

But Weil goes well beyond Herder in drawing moral and political consequences from this claim. Her insistence that a people must concede past crimes committed in its name, yet also seek to overcome those crimes without condemning the entire culture, anticipates the aim of the truth and reconciliation commissions—and more broadly, the concept of restorative justice—over the past quarter-century. Though making certain exceptions—most notably in the case of rapists who, Weil declared, merited the death penalty—she was viscerally opposed to retributive justice. Writing at a time when the desire for retribution overwhelmed the demand for reconciliation, she nevertheless insisted on the wisdom of the latter imperative. In general, she observed in her notebooks, the "apparatus of penal justice has been so contaminated with evil . . . that a condemnation is very often a transference of evil from the penal apparatus itself to the condemned man . . . Hardened criminals are the only people to whom the penal apparatus can do no harm. It does terrible harm to the innocent."[57] As for the postwar order, the pursuit of retribution would be not just needlessly provocative, but also pointless. In an argument that still shocks, Weil claimed that Hitler could not be punished. "He desired one thing alone, and he has it: to play a part in History. He can be killed, tortured, imprisoned, humiliated, but History will always be there to shield his spirit from all the ravages of suffering and death." In fact, she suggests that using retributive justice to punish Hitler amounts to confusing the symptom with the disease. "The only punishment capable of punishing Hitler, and deterring little boys thirsting for greatness in coming centuries from following his example, is such a total transformation of the meaning attached to greatness that he should thereby by excluded from it."[58]

✢✢

Picture for a moment the Western world's two most influential philosophers as Raphael did in his monumental painting,
School of Athens. In the middle of the canvas and striding toward
you are Plato and Aristotle. The younger and blue-robed Aristotle is gesturing earthward, while Plato, his onetime teacher,
gray-bearded and red-robed, is pointing heavenward. In her
writings, Weil fully embraced the latter and, at times, excoriated the former. When Weil does refer to Aristotle, frequently
she does so to dismiss him. In her notebooks, she was merciless:
"A village idiot, in the literal sense, who really loves the truth,
even when he only babbles, is in his thinking infinitely superior to Aristotle. He is infinitely nearer to Plato than Aristotle
ever was." In a late essay, she was a bit less severe, acknowledging that there is a "certain poetic beauty" to Aristotle's work,
all the while insisting that Plato and his disciples are "the true
masters of thought."

Yet Weil's scorn for Aristotle is surprising. After all, it was
Aristotle, the thinker pointing toward the soil, and not Plato,
with eyes only for the sky, who grasped the importance of roots.
He did so literally as well as figuratively. Though his student
and successor Theophrastus earned the title of "the father of
botany," Aristotle nevertheless wrote several works on plants.
(In fact, he bequeathed those works, since lost, along with the
rest of his library to Theophrastus when the latter took over
the Lyceum.) Based on surviving fragments, Aristotle's treatment of plants does appear rather abstract. Fittingly, though,
when he lectured on plants—or, for that matter, physics or
metaphysics—Aristotle did so while walking with his students
through the gardens of the Lyceum.

In his *Ethics*, in particular, Aristotle tilled the same soil
Weil would work two millennia later. For both the ancient Greek

and the modern French thinker, the core concern is what the former called *eudaimonia*. The word is often translated as "happiness"—the self-evident goal that, as Thomas Jefferson declared, we must be free to pursue. Yet, as historians like Garry Wills remind us, Jefferson and his contemporaries did not conceive of happiness the way most of us do today.[59] It has nothing to do with spending one's day at the races or one's night getting wasted, singing karaoke or sipping wine, collecting bobbleheads or connecting on social media. For the classically grounded Jefferson, it had everything to do with the work—pleasurable, but disciplined work—of becoming who you are. *Eudaimonia* is thus best translated as "human flourishing"—the ongoing and never-ending activity of fulfilling our potential, or capabilities, as human beings. For this reason, Aristotle (and Jefferson) insisted it is an ultimate good that we pursue as an end, not a means.

Aristotle makes clear that a human being, if isolated from or indifferent toward others, will never achieve this ultimate good, one that can be reached only in the company of others. *Eudaimonia* is, in fact, the end of all political activity. If a polis, or particular society, fails to enable its citizens to realize their potential or capability, it is less a true polis than a holding pen. "It belongs to the excellent legislator," Aristotle declares, "to see how a city, a family of human beings . . . will share in the good life and in the happiness that is possible for them."

In order for human beings to flourish, Aristotle held, a certain number of conditions had to be met. Not only must citizens be able to choose freely—a prerequisite for human dignity—but also they must be given the means and opportunities to flourish. In this respect, both Aristotle's and Weil's arguments are rehearsals for a modern-day movement known as the "capability approach." For the philosopher Martha Nussbaum, Aristotle's notion of *dunamis*, "human capability," maps largely onto the current work of capability theorists. She writes that, for Aristotle, any "decent political plan would seek to promote a range of diverse and incommensurable goods, involving the unfolding and development of distinct human abilities. Moreover, it must seek to promote them not just for some overall aggregate but for each and every citizen."[60] Though Nussbaum does not cite either Weil's name or her work, there are remarkable resemblances between Nussbaum's list of ten "central capabilities" and Weil's "fourteen needs" that open *The Need for Roots*. Whether called capabilities or needs, they constitute the bare minimum that a decent society must provide for all of its citizens.

For both Weil and Nussbaum, the foundations are necessarily material—namely, our physical needs. For Nussbaum, our capacity to live a long life, our access to adequate food and shelter, and our ability to go where we wish and be safe from physical harm, including sexual assault and domestic violence, are primordial.[61] Similarly, Weil observes that the needs of the body—which include protection against violence, as well as housing, clothing, heating, hygiene, and medical attention—precede those of the soul. Similarly, Weil insists, as does Nussbaum, upon the necessity of private property. This not only helps secure people from physical harm, but also helps nurture people's psychological and emotional needs. Every human being who works a plot of land or wields a set of tools soon comes to see them as extensions of themselves. As a result, Nussbaum notes, where "the feeling of appropriation doesn't coincide with any legally recognized ownership, men are continually exposed to extremely painful spiritual wrenches."[62]

Weil is at her most Aristotelian in her emphasis on education as the means for rooting the individual. In the concluding book of his *Politics*, Aristotle begins with the proposition that "the legislator should direct his attention above all to the education of youth, for the neglect of education does harm to state." Weil's writings on education reflect that same commitment. Equally important, there was her unwavering commitment to teaching not just her middle-class students, but also adult workers during weekends and evenings. Indeed, when it came to workers, Weil grasped that the neglect of their education did more than hobble their capacity to improve their lot; it also blocked their capacity to fundamentally change their lives. In order to accomplish the latter, reading revolutionary tracts and manifestos was no more useful than was reading *Marie-Claire*. Instead, she believed a manual laborer could, given the right teacher, better grasp certain "difficult" texts than could, say, a manager. "A workman who bears the anguish of unemployment deep in the very marrow of his bones, would understand the feelings of Philoctetus when his bow is taken away from him, and the despair with which he stares at his powerful hands. He would also understand that Electra is hungry, which a bourgeois, except just at present, is absolutely incapable of understanding."[63]

Is it really impossible, though, for a bourgeois to respond sympathetically to the vulnerability and abandonment experienced by Philoctetes? After all, the life of the young man who ultimately saves him, Neoptolemus, was no less privileged. And while a bourgeois might not worry about his next meal— except, as Weil notes, in occupied France—is he truly incapable of empathizing with those who do have such worries? In this instance, Weil builds a categorical claim on dubious foundations. Having worked in factories and on farms, and having imposed upon herself the same food rations as those imposed on the French, her own suffering, as well as her suffering for others, risks making her insufferable.

Yet her despair is also earned. Those same experiences buffered Weil against false hopes and pat proposals. With piercing clarity, she knows that even if workers had time enough to read such works, their world could never provide emotional space enough to reflect upon them. The very nature of their working lives—numbed by noise, dulled by repetition, anguished by insecurity—leaves little, if any, emotional space to engage these works. They are no less slaves than those who built the Parthenon. "To be free and sovereign, as a thinking being, for one hour or two, and a slave for the rest of the day, is such an agonizing spiritual quartering that it is almost impossible not to renounce . . . the highest forms of thought."[64]

⁂

"The highest forms of thought"—with this phrase, Weil signals a shift from the needs of the body to the needs of the soul. Though she does not make this explicit, these latter needs are historical, not theoretical in nature. How odd, then, that Weil does not treat the study of history at length in any of her works, though she certainly does not treat it with the same scorn that Aristotle reserves for the subject. When it comes to the ancient Greek historians, Weil knew them well, making a point of rereading the works of Herodotus and Thucydides—as well as that most Greek of Roman historians, Tacitus—as war loomed over Europe.[65] And yet, apart from occasional references (for example, Weil cites Thucydides's "Melian dialogue" as an example of force in human affairs), the historians are mostly walk-ons in her writings.

And yet, she insists upon the invaluable role played by the past in the life of a people. Developing Aristotle's assumption that we are not just political animals, but also social animals, Weil declares that the past is a vital source of meaning and purpose. The teaching of history, however, is not as a mere "summary of dates and landmarks." Instead, the past must be taught as tragedy portrayed it to the Greeks—as a visceral apprehension of truths that run deeper and darker than mere events. "Facts must not only be correct . . . but must be shown in their true perspective relatively to good and evil." The historian must not just present the past as it really was ("A tissue of base and cruel acts in the midst of which a few drops of purity sparkle at long intervals"), but seek out the "indirect testimony" for those "drops of purity."[66]

Though academic historians in her day or our own would smile at such claims, Weil believed issues of morality could no more be divorced from the writing of history than they could from the writing of literature. If historians are indifferent to virtue, they risk encouraging viciousness—or, equally unwelcome, skepticism or cynicism. In 1941, she sent a letter on this point to the literary journal *Cahiers du sud*, then embroiled in a debate over one of the oft-cited reasons for France's defeat— the decadence of French literature. Predictably, Weil refused to let writers off the hook: "Writers do not have to be professors of morals, but they do have to give expression to the human condition . . . When literature becomes deliberately indifferent to the opposition of good and evil, it betrays its function and has no pretense to excellence."[67]

Moreover, a community's ties to the past must be protected for the very same reason that a tree's roots in the earth must be protected: once those roots are torn up, death follows. Weil insists upon the unique character of each and every society, grounded in a congeries of events and experiences specific to it alone. As a result, the consequences of separating it from its particular grounding necessarily spell disaster. "Just as there are certain culture-beds for certain microscopic animals, certain types of soil for certain plants," Weil suggests, "so there is a certain part of the soul in everyone and certain ways of thought and action communicated from one person to another which can only exist in a national setting, and disappear when a country is destroyed."[68]

But rootedness does not exist in space alone. To be rooted means to belong to a community that spans time as well as territory; to be rooted means to participate in the life of that community; to be rooted, finally, means to preserve, as Weil writes, "certain particular treasures of the past and certain particular expectations of the future."[69] In this respect, the rapport between such passages and the writings of present-day communitarians seems nearly seamless. Just as the latter group have challenged John Rawls's conception of the individual in his classic *A Theory of Justice*—namely, that "each person possesses an inviolability founded on justice that even the welfare of society as a whole cannot override"—so too did Weil repudiate personalism, a philosophical movement during the interwar period that insisted, like Rawls, on the independence and interiority of the self.[70] And just as Weil argues that the humanness of the individual depends upon rootedness, so too do communitarian theorists believe that the true self is an "embedded self."

As thinkers like Charles Taylor, Michael Sandel, and Amitai Etzioni—to name just three of communitarianism's leading advocates—have variously argued, the Rawlsian conception of the individual is logically rigorous, but fatally misconceived. To portray the individual self as sovereign, existing outside of or separate from society, is as fictitious as the "natural man" that Jean-Jacques Rousseau gives us in his *Second Discourse*. Rousseau's contemporary critics, such as David Hume and Edmund Burke, pointed out that such a man could never have existed; communitarian thinkers make the same criticism of Rawls's "inviolable self." We are always already social creatures, our selves formed and informed by the community into which we are born and in which we are raised. There is, quite simply, no self without society. As a result, as political theorists would have it, we are necessarily "embedded" or "embodied" selves. Sandel underscores the moral consequences of the Rawlsian worldview.

"The weakness of the liberal conception of freedom is bound up with its appeal. If we understand ourselves as free and independent selves, unbound by moral ties we haven't chosen, we can't make sense of a range of moral and political obligations that we commonly recognize, even prize."[71] As Weil's list of needs and obligations reveals, she could not have agreed more.

⁂

In 1791, a struggling pamphleteer and playwright, Olympe de Gouges, published a work that shouldered its way onto the stage of history. A feminist *avant la lettre*, Gouges took the *Declaration of the Rights of Man and Citizen*, written two years earlier, and gave both the title and contents a revolutionary tweak. With the *Declaration of the Rights of Woman and Citizeness*, Gouges declared that if liberty and equality were to be realized, then the notion of fraternity was not enough. If rights were truly universal, they had to go beyond brotherhood and apply to *citoyennes* as well as *citoyens*. As her opening line announces: "Woman, awake: the tocsin of reason resounds through the whole universe: discover your rights!" In the end, the tocsin of unreason resounded louder. Gouges ended her days by offering to defend Louis XVI at his trial—an offer, she explained, spurred by her desire to show that women were as capable as men of "heroism and generosity." For her opposition to the Terror, she exited from the same bloody stage, via the guillotine, as did her erstwhile client.

Though Weil makes no mention of Gouges, the two women shared certain traits. The latter's dramatic offer to defend the king reflects the same understanding of symbolism and sacrifice as does the former's proposal to be parachuted onto a battlefield. Moreover, Gouges appreciates, as does Weil, the importance of tying duties to rights. But Weil would also find that, in this regard, Gouges's appreciation did not go as far as it should. By 1943, it was no longer a matter of dusting off the *Declaration of the Rights of Woman and Citizeness*, not to mention its male-centered predecessor. Instead, by swapping out a single word from the title, Weil proposed a radically different declaration, one based upon the *needs*, and not the rights, of all citizens.

In the list of fourteen "needs of the soul" with which she begins *The Need for Roots*, Weil offers both the familiar—liberty, equality, and freedom of opinion—and the unfamiliar, such as order, hierarchism, and honor. Each of these needs, Weil declares, entails obligation on the part of others. With the same self-assurance shown by the writers of the first declaration in 1789, who insisted upon the natural, inalienable, and sacred rights of man, Weil asserts: "Duty towards the human being as such—that alone is eternal."

But where the preamble to the 1789 declaration identifies "ignorance, neglect, or contempt of man [as] the sole cause of public calamities," Weil has her doubts. The simple fact that rights go unrecognized suggests that they are "not worth very much"—a truth grasped by authoritarians on both sides of the Atlantic. In her essay "Human Personality," Weil presents an unexpected illustration of her point. If someone tries to force a farmer to sell his eggs at a lower price, the farmer will reply: "I've the right to keep my eggs if you refuse to pay the asking price." But now imagine a young girl who is forced into prostitution. "She will not talk about her rights," Weil observes. "In such a situation, the word would sound ludicrously inadequate."[72]

The dated wording and setting lend the impression that the negotiation over eggs is akin to a Saturday-morning trip to our local farmer's market. But Weil was undoubtedly thinking of her own life during the "*exode*," watching desperate Parisians trying to buy eggs from farms along the escape route. Less dated, though, is her allusion to a young girl forced into a brothel. Sex trafficking is, of course, a global plague, one battled by numerous human rights organizations. While Weil would admire their dedication, she would also wonder if they grasp the full extent of the crime. To frame sex trafficking as a violation of a human right, Weil believes, and not a violation of a human need is to miss the enormity of the act. For Weil, rights are the reflection of the modern, commercial, and contractual societies in which they were conceived. As a result, to describe what is done to this young girl as a violation of her rights is to obscure rather than clarify what is at stake—which is to say, her personhood.

In her merciless treatment of rights, Weil once again treats the making of fine distinctions as a dereliction of moral duty, or a refuge for the intellectually and morally fainthearted. At the same time, however, her stark claims oblige us to rethink the nature of obligation. Weil is not indifferent to rights; instead, she holds that they do not always meet the demands of true justice. For this reason, while the preamble to the 1789 declaration insists "that ignorance, neglect, or contempt of the rights of man are the sole cause of public calamities," Weil is not convinced. They may well contribute to a society's disarray, but the fact that they go unrecognized suggests they are "not worth very much." This brutal truth has been repeatedly hammered home by the behavior of the Trump administration in the United States. At the same time, we have seen time and again the truth of Weil's corollary—namely, that obligations to our fellow human beings always "remain independent of conditions."

This goes to the heart of Weil's enterprise: the corollary to another's needs is our obligation to recognize them, regardless of conditions. No doubt she often reflected on this moral imperative as she pored over the reports sent by the Resistance movements in France, burdened by the "terrible responsibility" both they and the Free French had assumed. So much more was at stake than the defeat of Nazi Germany. The traditional understanding of rights and duties, of the nation and nationalism, also had to be defeated, a task Weil described as "nothing less than a question of refashioning the soul of the country."[73] Compounding the difficulty, she warned, was the miasma of mendacity that had settled on France: "Our age is so poisoned by lies that it converts everything it touches into a lie."[74] This was the work not just of the Vichy regime, but also of the Third Republic that had preceded it. As evidence, Weil cited the education of the nation's youth. Children have been taught, she wrote, that "things concerning the country . . . have a degree of importance which sets them apart from other things." But here's the rub: "It is precisely in regard to those things that justice, consideration for others, and obligations assigning limits to ambitions and appetites never get mentioned."[75]

The answer to uprootedness, for Weil, lay in embracing one of its principal causes: "The world requires at the present time a new patriotism. And it is now that this inventive effort must be made, just when patriotism is something which is causing bloodshed." The nation was an imperfect vehicle for a shared sense of identity and meaning, but it was the best on offer. The nation, and the nation alone, would play "the part which constitutes the supreme mission of society toward the individual human being, namely, maintaining throughout the present the links with the past and the future." In her diagnosis of the modern predicament, Weil warned that a renewed emphasis on universal rights was inadequate to the challenge at hand.

* *

Many signs remind me that the end of 2019 is nearly here. The afternoon sun to which our vacationing children awaken is pale and casts long shadows of the bare branches of our trees. Also, our mailbox fills every day with fund-raising missives from organizations like Human Rights Watch, Human Rights Without Frontiers, and the Human Rights League—but we never hear from, say, a Human Obligations Watch. To be honest, this comes as a relief. I find it is so much easier to write a bunch of checks than to spend a bunch of hours in food banks or refugee shelters in the company of those whose needs are not being met by our society or, yes, by myself.

Weil would find me wanting. But she would also find our century wanting. One of the reasons there is no Human Obligations Watch request in my mailbox is because no such organization exists. Yet, this absence is something of a historical anomaly. Until the twentieth century, observes the historian Samuel Moyn, the question of obligation and duty held center stage in juridical and philosophical debates, while rights were very much a sideshow. Now that these roles are reversed, he writes, the consequences are significant. "Human rights themselves wither when their advocates fail to cross the border into the language of duty; insofar as compliance with norms on paper is sought, the bearers of duties have to be identified and compelled to assume their burden."[76]

Weil would certainly agree with such a claim. But she would also argue that it does not go nearly far enough. The imperative of obligations and duties, Weil insisted, must be anchored in a place that will always hold fast. Such a place will be found not by digging deep, but instead by clambering high.

CHAPTER FIVE

The Good, the Bad,
and the Godly

*Those who no longer believe in God do not believe in
nothing. Far worse, they now believe in anything.*

IRIS MURDOCH

*The simplicity that makes fictional good a pallid
thing that cannot get a glance from us is an
unfathomable marvel in real good.*

SIMONE WEIL

Weil's searing experience in Spain shattered what remained of
her physical health. It might also have opened her to the possibility that politics alone could not fully grasp the human condition. Prior to Spain, Weil had already glimpsed that possibility
when, following her factory experience, she traveled to Portugal
with her parents in the hope of recovering her strength. When
she left her parents at their hotel and wandered into a fishing
village, she stumbled across the cortège of women performing
the rituals for their patron saint's day. Weil later observed that
her own suffering, or *malheur*, resonated with the suffering,
framed by Christian faith, she saw and heard that night.

This incident on the Portuguese coast proved to be a rehearsal
of sorts for Weil's slow and never quite completed embrace of
Roman Catholicism. Come 1937 and another family trip, this
time to Italy, she underwent a second conversion experience.

Visiting a Romanesque chapel in Assisi, she felt something "stronger than I was" that forced her to her knees, and there, for the first time in her life, she began to pray. The climactic experience, however, took place the following year in France, at the Benedictine abbey of Solesmes, when, her head in the vise of a migraine, Weil attended a liturgical service during which "the Passion of Christ entered into my being once and for all."[1]

During the five years between her rebirth at Solesmes and her death in Ashford, Weil engaged in a brilliant and often bruising dialogue with Christianity. In June 1941, when she was living in Marseille and collaborating with the Resistance journal *Cahiers du témoignage chrétien*, she encountered the first of two men who became her key Catholic interlocutors. The Dominican priest Joseph-Marie Perrin shared a number of traits with Weil: he was in his midthirties, physically frail, and intellectually formidable. As already noted, he was also active in refugee circles and Resistance work, serving at *Témoignage chrétien*—an activity that forced him to flee Marseille and go underground in 1943—when not serving as confessor at the city's Dominican convent. Paradoxically, Perrin and Weil had little in common when it came to Judaism. A philo-Semite and promoter of interfaith dialogue, the Dominican father failed to fully comprehend Weil's hostility to the Hebrew Bible and Jewish faith, just as he failed to convince her that her interpretations were often mistaken or misconceived.

After their initial interview, Weil and Perrin met several times in Marseille, and they continued their conversations through correspondence when Weil left for New York in mid-1942. Weil's letters to Perrin form the bulk of *Attente de dieu*, Weil's "spiritual autobiography" first published in 1950, soon followed by the English translation, *Waiting for God*. To read the letters is to be unnerved: the rawness of the personal revelations, rigor of the intellectual insights, and resoluteness of the spiritual longing always catch the reader on the back foot. Or by the throat. There is a constant thrum of tension in Weil's relationship to Christianity, as she was pulled in opposite directions by the desire to surrender herself wholly to the Church and the indignation at so much of its history and dogma that prevented her from doing so. Although she came to embrace the faith, Weil was embarrassed by the institution; as she told Perrin, "I have not the slightest love for the Church in the strict sense of the word."[2] Appalled by a religion with universal claims that does not allow for the salvation of all humankind, she refused to separate herself from the fate of unbelievers. *Anathema sit*, the Church's sentence of banishment against heretics, filled Weil with horror. A tool of totalitarians, anathema obliterates the essence of human dignity: our intelligence to see the world as it is and act accordingly. Though Perrin failed to bring Weil inside the Church, Weil did bring him something else of value: two of her most original essays, "The Love of God and Affliction" and "Forms of the Implicit Love of God," which Perrin subsequently added to *Waiting for God*.

The second of Weil's interlocutors, as we earlier observed, was Gustave Thibon. This self-professed *paysan*, or peasant, was also an aspiring Catholic theologian. Supportive of Philippe Pétain and sympathetic to Vichy's worldview, Thibon became a house intellectual who took up their call for a return to the soil and faith. Not surprisingly, Thibon admired Charles Maurras's writing, even though he insisted that he never formally joined Action Française. Maurras returned the admiration, describing Thibon in 1942 as "incontestably the most brilliant of our young stars." Despite Thibon's predilections, Perrin, moved by Weil's intense desire to find manual work, asked if he would take her on as a field worker. After some hesitation, Thibon agreed to take on the refugee Jew.

At first, Thibon regretted his decision. When Weil arrived at his home in early August 1941, Thibon's reaction was decidedly mixed: "I had the impression of being face to face with an individual who was radically foreign to all my ways of thinking and feeling and . . . one who refused to make any concession whatever to the requirements and conventions of social life." His doubts deepened as Weil managed to complicate his simplest expectations. As we saw, Weil was unwilling to sleep under the same roof as the Thibons, plumping instead for a distant and decaying hut. Though she sat down for meals with Thibon and his wife, Weil ate very little, insisting it was a matter not of choice, but of rationing. When not throwing herself with her customary awkwardness into her manual tasks, Weil tutored Thibon in Greek, helping him work through Plato's *Phaedo*. Like Perrin, Thibon was eventually won over—seduced is not too powerful a word—by his farmhand's faith. He confessed his "veneration" for Weil, placing her in the ranks of Catholicism's greatest mystics. At the same time, he was not blind to her contradictions, noting that this "soul who wanted to be flexible to every movement of the divine will could not bear the course of events, or the kindness of friends, altering by one iota the positioning of the stakes with which she had marked the path of self-immolation."[3]

Just as Weil did with Perrin, so too with Thibon: shortly before she embarked for New York, she entrusted him with her writings. In this case, it was a dozen of her notebooks, the source for *Gravity and Grace*, the collection of passages that Thibon selected, introduced, and published shortly after the end of the war. Perhaps more than any of her other works, this volume has introduced successive generations of curious readers to Weil. This, in turn, poses certain problems that have sparked debates among scholars, long divided over Thibon's tendency to obscure Weil's inveterate doubts over Catholicism and underscore her anti-Jewish declarations. Moreover, by arranging these notes into separate batches and slapping a label on each of them, Thibon recasts Weil's thoughts as epigrams, identifying them with themes of his choosing, and not Weil's. While this is not the same order of misrepresentation that, say, Elisabeth Forster-Nietzsche committed in her editing of her brother's *Nachlass* (known to the world as *The Will to Power*), Thibon's framing of Weil's words needs to be kept in mind.

Weil's conversion experience was dramatic, but oddly redundant. Not that she was always a believer—far from it. Though she told Perrin she had decided in her youth to leave the question of God alone, Weil was not quite accurate. While most intellectuals on the French left disdained the Christian faith and despised the Catholic Church, Weil could not leave either the one or the other completely alone. She had long been drawn, in a vague and hesitant fashion, to both. Here as elsewhere, Weil was marked by Alain, who also conflicted on the subject of Christianity. Though he was dependably anticlerical, he was not an unbeliever. Instead, he always insisted that "God cannot *not* exist." Alain was, moreover, taken by the core tenets of the Christian faith, such as the crucifixion and virgin birth, and often used the phrase "saving my soul" when he lectured in class.[4] When still a student of Alain's, Weil drafted a paper on the nature of Christ's real presence at communion; in other papers and conversations she often quoted from the New Testament. She was also keen on touring cathedrals and churches, and once fell out with a classmate who had behaved poorly during their visit to Notre-Dame in Paris.[5]

But visits to churches and citations from scripture do not a conversion make. The true bridge between Weil's preconversion and postconversion lives was built not by the ancient Christians, but instead by the ancient Greeks. Especially after her mystical experiences in 1937–38, Weil insisted upon the seamless movement between Greek thought and Christian faith. "All Greek civilization is a search for bridges that relate human misery to divine perfection. Their art, which is incomparable, their poetry, their philosophy, the science which they invented ... are nothing but bridges. They invented the idea of mediation."[6] For Weil, Plato was the master builder. From her first class with Alain, which he devoted to Plato's dialogues and Balzac's novels, Weil's love for the philosopher remained steadfast. In the first line of her first essay, the young Weil announced: "Among Plato's finest thoughts are those he had by reflecting on myths."[7] With her own students, she always returned to Plato, as she did in her notes and articles, insisting that the ancient Athenian's works "are more useful, even today, to anyone who wishes to understand human nature than all the books on psychology put together."[8]

As late as 1941, Weil continued to assert that "nothing surpasses Plato."[9] How could it be otherwise? With his parable of the cave, revealing a reality more real than our own reality, Plato's thought was literally unsurpassable. In her love of the parable, what Weil latched onto in Plato was not what drew most of her fellow philosophers—his dialectical reasoning and political theorizing—but instead what they mostly shunned: his love of myths. Through these myths, Plato offered a method of spiritual orientation, a philosophy devoid of doctrine and devoted to the notion of *metaxu*—a metaphysical Checkpoint Charlie between the worldly and otherworldly. Hence her insistence that idealism, at least when it comes to Plato (if not Kant), "is not a philosophical doctrine, but the expression of our very first experience."[10] If this sounds rather like mysticism, it is because it is. Weil makes no bones about it: "My interpretation is that Plato is an authentic mystic, perhaps the father of western mysticism."[11]

※

While the claim that Plato is the father of Western mysticism might invite debate, this would not be the case for the claim that Isaac Luria is the father of Jewish mysticism. The sixteenth-century founder of the Kabbalist school in Safed, Luria developed a system of thought, written down by his followers, that was eagerly embraced by the large and prosperous Jewish communities that, in 1492, were banished from their native Spain and Portugal. There had been many earlier expulsions of Jews in Europe—for instance, the French expulsion in 1306—but the Spanish instance was uniquely traumatic. "Precisely because this expulsion was not the first but, in a vital sense, the last," observed the historian Yosef Yerushalmi, "it was felt to have altered the face of Jewry and of history itself . . . That the largest and proudest Jewry in Europe had been uprooted was tragic enough. The larger significance of the Spanish Expulsion lay in the fact that, as a result, Western Europe had been emptied of Jews."[12]

There was, however, another profoundly significant consequence of the exodus of Spanish Jews. At first, it spurred the effort of some medieval Jewish scholars to make historical sense of the event. Somehow the expulsion, though seismic, could nevertheless be grasped as a natural, and not supernatural, event. Yet this effort soon petered out, yielding to a radically different and daring interpretation firmly rooted in the supernatural. By the end of the sixteenth century, the promise of Jewish historiography gave way to the pathos of Jewish mysticism, a movement on which Luria left his momentous and mind-bending stamp.

At the heart of Lurianic mysticism is the notion of *Tsim-tsum*. While the word means "concentration" in Hebrew, Luria invested it with the meaning of "retreat" or "withdrawal." Taking issue with Jewish tradition, Luria insisted that God did not concentrate his essence and power into a single point; instead, He more or less decamped from this same point. The cosmos could only come into existence if God first removed himself from this celestial scene. The world's presence, for Luria, is conceivable only through God's absence. As the scholar Gershom Scholem writes: "God was compelled to make room for the world by, as it were, abandoning a region within Himself, a kind of mystical primordial space from which He withdrew in order to return to it in the act of creation and revelation."[13] In a word, God uprooted himself. By clearing the ground for his creation, He severed part of himself. God's self-imposed expulsion was the otherworldly reflection of the worldly expulsion suffered by Spanish Jewry in Luria's day.

Or, for that matter, in Weil's own day. There is no sign, in her letters or journals, that Weil had ever read Luria or was aware of the Kabbalic strand of Jewish theology. Given Weil's innocence of this aspect of Jewish thought, the parallels between her notion of *décréation* and Luria's concept of *Tsimtsum* are all the more astonishing. Both were conceived at times of singular social upheaval and existential fears. But both were also conceived as alternatives to secular interpretations of these two traumatic events.

For Weil, God shows his love to his creation by withdrawing from it. Indeed, God has no choice but to do so, since He cannot coexist with a cosmos filled with inanimate and animate things—humankind included. As Weil observed, "God could create only by hiding himself. Otherwise there would be nothing but himself."[14] Yet God folds himself into eight, as it were, only to have us, his creation, unfold him at our own expense. In an especially chilling passage, Weil announces that "he who gives us being loves in us our consent not to be . . . Our being is nothing other than the will that we should consent not to be. He is forever begging from us the being which he gives. And he gives it so as to beg it from us."[15] In Weil's scheme, God is at best neurotic, at worst sociopathic; a divinity who has wrought a cosmos

He wishes He never had and filled it with residents who should wish they never were. "Relentless necessity, wretchedness, distress, the crushing burden of poverty and of labor which wears us out, cruelty, torture, violent death, constraint, disease—all these constitute divine love. It is God who in love withdraws from us so that we can love him. For if we were exposed to the direct radiance of his love, without the protection of space, time and matter, we should be evaporated like water in the sun; there would not be enough 'I' in us to make it possible to surrender the 'I' for love's sake. Necessity is the screen set between God and us so that we can be. It is for us to pierce through the screen so that we can cease to be."[16]

Weil's drive to unmake herself drew her to others who, she believed, shared the same desire. This was the case for the Cathars, the medieval religious sect that had caught Weil's attention when she lived in Marseille. The Cathars believed that an evil deity had created the material world, while a good deity governed the immaterial realm. In this cosmic struggle, the sect's spiritual elite, known as the *perfecti* or "good men," did their share by leading lives of extreme physical abnegation.[17] Weil believed, as she wrote to Déodat Roché, an amateur historian of Catharism, that the Cathars channeled the mystical genius of pre-Roman antiquity: "They alone really escaped the coarseness of mind and baseness of heart which were disseminated over vast territories by the Roman dominion."[18]

Identifying so deeply with the Cathars, Weil romanticized not only their teachings and practices, but also the culture and history of Languedoc. In a similar manner, Weil eagerly bought into the mythologizing of another, much later revolt against imperial oppression: the Arab rising for independence that was, in part, led by the twentieth-century *perfectus* T. E. Lawrence. In a letter to her friend Jean Posternak, she urged him to read *Seven Pillars of Wisdom*, describing its author as an "authentic hero" who was not just a scholar and artist, but "a kind of saint as well."[19] While Weil was engrossed by Lawrence's account of his role in the revolt, she was carried away by the life he led after the war. More than refusing the rewards his fame offered, he insisted on undoing, perhaps even decreating that fame. Enlisting in the Royal Air Force, Lawrence changed his name, first to Ross then Shaw, and cultivated—perhaps a bit too self-consciously—the anonymity he had lost. He was indifferent to money, keen on manual labor, and prone to punishing his body. Weil perceived these traits, so close to her own, and praised them to those who would listen. In a letter to Lawrence's editor, David Garnett, she wrote that what she found most compelling were Lawrence's "years of voluntary suffering and degradation . . . Indeed, he seems still more human and at the same time greater in his slavery than in his glory."[20]

As so often with Weil, her claim on behalf of decreation compels as powerfully as it repels. In this instance of extreme interpersonal dysfunction at an intergalactic dimension, it is no clearer why her God would accept to create us than why we would accept to continue this bizarre family dynamic. How different this life-denying interpretation is from Luria's life-affirming insistence that we can make whole a wounded God by being present in, not absent from, the world. Nevertheless, if we dig deeply enough, we will find a powerful truth at the core of Weil's claim. While we might well be overpowered or undermined by forces coursing through the physical world, our principal nemesis is the force that courses inside each and every one of us: the "I." But in order to break this thralldom, do we need to turn to Weil's Christian mysticism? Not at all, believed one brilliant admirer of Weil, the Anglo-Irish novelist and philosopher Iris Murdoch.

⁂

"Have I come to the end of the path which started many years ago when I first read Simone Weil and saw a far-off light in the forest?"[21] In this journal entry from 1968, Murdoch harkened back to the war years when, as a philosophy student at Oxford, she first discovered Weil's writings. By the end of the decade, when she had become one of Oxford's youngest dons and was on the verge of becoming one of England's most promising writers, Murdoch began to introduce Weil's works to English readers. She also drew Weil into her own reflections on the nature of the moral life—a life that, as she wrote many years later, needed to be inhabited by the thinker. What especially drew Murdoch to Weil, both then and toward the end of her life, was the French thinker's stubborn pursuit of the Good. For Weil, faith was the pursuit of the Good by other means; for Murdoch, the Good was her means for remaining tethered to this world.

While always relevant, the question of goodness was especially acute in the immediate aftermath of World War II. Between 1944 and 1946, Murdoch, recently graduated from Oxford, went to work in war-torn Belgium and Austria with the United Nations Relief and Rehabilitation Administration. Not only did she encounter scenes of utter devastation and despair—nothing short, she reported, of the "total breakdown of human society"—but she also met the young Jean-Paul Sartre. Enchanted by his person and principles—diving into his work, she exclaimed it was "the real thing"—Murdoch was perfectly situated to ride the great wave of existentialism churning across the Channel. Fluent in French, she explored the works of Albert Camus, Simone de Beauvoir, and Maurice Merleau-Ponty, and, in her lucid and sinewy language, introduced these thinkers to an Anglo-American audience.

Nevertheless, Murdoch's fascination with this strand of French thought faded. By the late 1950s, she had become disenchanted with existentialism's more flamboyant claims, especially in regard to radical freedom. In the end, she declared, it was not "the philosophy we need." Instead, the philosophy the world now needed, she believed, was the one that existentialism and the postwar analytic turn had left in the dust. Though intrigued by the writings of Ludwig Wittgenstein, Murdoch nevertheless, and very much against philosophical current, declared herself a Platonist. Already, during the war years, she had discovered that "there was no wide consideration of [Plato], he was simply misunderstood. I learnt nothing of value about him as an undergraduate (he was regarded as 'literature'!)."[22]

What Murdoch found most compelling in Plato's thought was his claim that concepts like "Beauty" and "Justice" and "the Good" are transcendental yet real, offering eternal standards for our own activities. As Plato insisted, once you truly perceive "the Good," you have no choice but to act on it. But Weil's twist to the notion of attention—an act that, as we have seen, demands the dismantling of the "I"—invited Murdoch to rethink the nature of goodness. Though briefly tempted by Christianity in the 1940s, Murdoch could not follow Weil as far as aligning the Good with God, being unable or unwilling to cross over from Platonism to deism. (Some critics nevertheless believed she did cross the line, prompting Murdoch to quip that her philosophy tended to end up as theology—a problem, she added, as she didn't believe in God.) God, Murdoch concluded, was what she called a "jumped-up" term—"a false intermediary invented by human selfishness to make the difficult task of virtue look easier and more attractive."[23] As a result, she added a second "o" to "God" and rooted "the Good" at the center of a moral person's activity.

Nevertheless, in offering a Platonism for our age, Murdoch refined the architect's original plans by moving the concept of the Good from the transcendental to the personal plane. Or, more accurately, by insisting on constant movement between these two planes. Murdoch does not question that the Good exists outside of one's private world—that it is real. What she does question is what we usually understand by "reality" and "realism." The only reality worth its salt is the one where we hold the salt shaker—one that depends, in other words, on the working of our minds. Rather than conceiving of realism as a photographic replica of the real world, Murdoch argues that realism means that we inevitably introduce value into the world we confront. When we attend rightly to the world—as do great artists or great souls—we see it as it truly is.

If only it were so easy. Getting in our way and blocking our vision are our very own selves. What makes the work of attention so hard, for Murdoch, is the "fat relentless ego."[24] She identifies the enemy, personal fantasy, as nothing more than "the tissue of self-aggrandizing and consoling wishes and dreams that prevents one from seeing what is there outside one." In her formulation, the crux of the moral life is not our willing to do good, but instead our *seeing* the good. By pulling off the filter of selfish concerns, we wrest ourselves from what Murdoch calls the "mire" of egotistical desires, and look at the world and others as they really are. One consequence of unfettering our vision is that we find that our self becomes a smaller and less compelling object.

In her philosophical essays, Murdoch explicitly acknowledges her debt to Weil, whom she calls "that admirable Platonist."[25] Moral philosophy and religion, she believed, share the same nemesis and offer techniques for snapping our ties to our relentlessly pushing and pulling selves. Yet Murdoch took Weil's notion of force and placed it inside rather than outside our own selves. What is the id, after all, but a force indifferent not just to the well-being of others, but ultimately to the well-being of its possessor? We are, Murdoch suggested, "largely mechanical creatures, the slaves of relentlessly strong selfish forces the nature of which we scarcely comprehend . . . There are perhaps in the case of every human being insuperable psychological barriers to goodness."[26] For this reason, moral philosophy's one and only task is to find a way to purify and reorient this "energy which is naturally selfish in such a way that when moments of choice arrive we shall be sure of acting rightly."[27]

This is where the Good enters. It is the transcendental reality that lights the path to "unselfing"—a term whose therapeutic character Murdoch understandably preferred to Weil's apocalyptic "decreation." The Good invites us to cast away our own self, allowing us to see and respond to fellow human beings in all of their subjectivity. To seek the Good is nothing more nor less, she announced, than "the attempt to pierce the veil of selfish consciousness and join the world as it really is." A stirring claim, but one to which Murdoch quickly added a proviso: "it is an empirical fact about human nature that this attempt cannot be entirely successful."[28]

But is she right? Consider the case of André Trocmé. The Protestant pastor of the French hamlet of Le Chambon-sur-Lignon, Trocmé, with his fellow villagers, managed to save the lives of about three thousand Jewish refugees during the Occupation. Several years later, when the American philosopher Philip Hallie visited the village, he kept asking the locals why they did what they did. Did they not know the great risks? Were they not more concerned about their own lives, or those of their own loved ones? The villagers, in turn, were at a loss over how to answer Hallie's persistent questions. Why the fuss? one replied. We did what we had to do. This was an echo of the simple, yet staggering answer Trocmé gave the police when they demanded he hand over the Jews he was hiding: "We do not know what a Jew is. We know only men." In the end, Le Chambon-sur-Lignon became a place of goodness not because Trocmé and his parishioners read the great moral thinkers, but instead because they knew how to read the world. Their vision was clear because their egos were, if not suppressed, at least contained. They knew the place that rescuing fellow human beings must take in their lives. To tweak an observation Murdoch originally made about scholars: "A pastor has great merits. But a pastor who is also a good man knows not only his subject but the proper place of his subject in the whole of his life."

Albert Camus would have agreed. He lived at Le Panelier, a hamlet just outside Le Chambon, during this same period. Having gone to Le Panelier as a cure for his worsening tuberculosis, he did not participate in the Resistance activities at Chambon. Indeed, it is unclear if Camus was even aware of these activities or, if he was, how much he knew. But it was at Le Panelier that Camus took notes for *The Plague* and gave a name to his novel's clear-eyed and truth-telling narrator: Doctor Rieux. Perhaps it was simply a coincidence that the name of Chambon's own doctor was Riou. Still, it is telling that Rieux makes a *profession de foi* worthy of Weil and Murdoch when he defines his job as "a matter of lucidly recognizing what had to be recognized; of dispelling extraneous shadows and doing what needed to be done."[29]

Murdoch, who thought as highly of the novel as she did of its author, described Rieux as a "Christian *manqué*." It is hard not to smile at Murdoch's description, since she herself invited the same moniker. But it is less that Murdoch fell short of Christianity than that she never fell far from a certain kind of Platonism—the very sort she always associated with Weil. What Murdoch took from this "admirable Platonist" was the conviction that seeing well is tantamount to doing well. Discerning the Good—the way the world truly is—whittles down our range of choices to just one. As she explains, "I can only choose within the world that I can see, in the moral sense of 'see' which implies that clear vision is a result of moral imagination and moral effort."[30] For both Murdoch and Weil, to see clearly is to act coherently. What appear as two distinct activities are, in effect, one.

Neither Weil nor Murdoch thought much of the Delphic imperative "Know thyself." For both of them, the true imperative was to know others. Rather than picking away at the self, far better to pick one's way through the world. It is the quality of our attachments to what exists outside of what Murdoch called the "fantasy mechanism," or self, that exemplifies goodness, and not the scrutiny of the self. Hence, the philosophical ground zero of the Good for both thinkers is the parable of the cave in Plato's *Republic*. It is a mistake, Weil declared, to think that "the metaphor of the cave relates to knowledge and that sight signifies the intelligence. The sun is the good. Sight is then the faculty which is in relationship with the good."[31] Similarly, Murdoch identifies the Good, and not knowledge, with the sun, the source that allows the "moral pilgrim" emerging from the cave to truly see the real world.[32] Just as with the sun, so too with the Good: we cannot look directly at either, but both allow us to directly see the world.

Inevitably, Murdoch's notion of the Good might seem little more than the reluctant addition of another "o" to "God." Believers might wonder why Murdoch bothers, especially as her Platonic model does not come equipped with the standard features of the Christian model, including a personal relationship with the Maker and a warranty good for all eternity. Murdoch confessed that she herself had, at times, doubts about insisting upon the Good as our central point of reflection. Yet, she also maintained that there is something in the "serious attempt to look compassionately at human things which automatically suggests that 'there is more than this.'" While Murdoch acknowledged the difficulty in pinning down what this "more" is, she kept returning to the Good. Just as transcendence in religion leads to God, transcendence in morality must lead to the Good—a claim rooted not in psychology, but in reality. Convinced that goodness is a form of realism, Murdoch declares that a good person living in isolation makes no more sense than a living tree suspended in midair. Both the tree and person need to be rooted, the one to live and the other to achieve the good. "A good man must know certain things about his surroundings, most obviously the existence of other people and their claims. The chief enemy of excellence in morality (and also in art) is personal fantasy: the tissue of self-aggrandizing and consoling wishes and dreams which prevents one from seeing what is there outside one."[33]

✠

Such wishes and dreams blind us to seeing not only what is outside our selves, but also what is outside our group. For Weil, few institutions better exemplified this truth than political parties. In a proposal that would have pleased General de Gaulle, had he read it, Weil called for the abolition of all political parties. She argued that parties, regardless of their ideological coloration, share three basic traits. They are dedicated to nurturing collective passions, designed to exercise collective pressure upon the minds of their members, and devoted to their collective self-preservation. These traits, in turn, make it nigh impossible for the individual members of political parties to think and act as individuals.

Imagine, Weil asks, a political candidate who declares: "Whenever I shall have to examine any political or social issue, I swear I will absolutely forget that I am the member of a certain political group; my sole concern will be to ascertain what should be done in order to best serve the public interest and justice."[34] Such a claim would elicit either a puzzled frown or loud guffaw on the part of other party members, all the while sentencing the candidate to censure or exile. From her unforgiving analysis, Weil draws unsparing conclusions. If a political party is, as she writes, "a marvelous mechanism which, on the national scale, ensures that not a single mind can attend to the effort of perceiving, in public affairs, what is good, just and true," then the party has no place in the public square.

You find this claim to be undemocratic? Weil would then remind you that democracy is not a good in, of, and by itself. What would you think of democracy, she asks, if it had been the Weimar Republic, not Nazi Germany, that "put the Jews in concentration camps, and cruelly tortured them to death?" Such a notion, Weil adds, "is by no means far-fetched."[35] After all, it was republican, not Vichy, France that built the concentration camps along its own southern border for Spanish refugees from the Spanish Civil War, in which she had fought. Soon after, these same camps interned Jewish refugees from Hitler's war against them.

That democracies would abide concentration camps is shocking, but not surprising. No less shocking, but perhaps more surprising to our ears, Weil insists that democracy is not an end, but instead a means. It exists, quite simply, to achieve the good. If it achieves only the bad, it must then be discarded. The problem, of course, is that, given the dominance of parties, which define and distill democratic politics, the bad inevitably wins out.

Could it be any different when politicians represent party interests rather than the public interest? One should think what one thinks, Weil argues, "not because one happens to be French or Catholic or Socialist, but simply because the irresistible light of evidence forces one to think this and not that."[36] Yet this had become impossible, Weil believed, in an age of mass politics and communication, comparing interwar radio and tabloids to "cocaine" that distorts and degrades the individual's ability to attend to the world and to others. (How quaint a notion in our own age, in which the feedback loops between political parties and cable TV news are the intellectual equivalent of our opioid crisis.)

At the end of her proposal, Weil laments that, nearly everywhere, citizens no longer think, but instead "they take sides: for or against." Her contemporaries had swapped the activity of the mind and the acknowledgment of complexity for the inanity of prejudice and the insistence upon simplicity. What Weil diagnosed as this "intellectual leprosy" is hardly unique to her time and place. Now, as then, nothing is more comfortable, Weil announced, "than not having to think"—or, in what amounts to the same thing, to think collectively, which is the lifeblood of political parties.[37] Few organizations, Weil concluded, are better suited for suffocating all sense of truth and goodness, for few organizations are more adept at exerting "a collective pressure upon people's minds. This pressure is very real; it is not only displayed; it is professed and proclaimed." Weil's conclusion is as relevant today as it was in her own day: "This should horrify us, but we are already too much accustomed to it."[38]

⁂

"How much time do you devote each day to thinking?" During her stay at Middlesex Hospital, Weil sometimes asked the attending nurses this question. Although the nurses may have been puzzled by the question, there is a good chance they were taken with the questioner. Like others from modest social circumstances, the nurses seem to have had Weil's full attention. (And, like others in positions of authority, the doctors were often left bewildered and bothered by this impossible patient. The presiding physician, Dr. Bennett, who was unable to persuade her to undergo treatment for her tubercular lungs or even to eat her meals, later declared that Weil was "the most difficult patient he had ever encountered.")[39]

But these nurses, one suspects, were not the ones Weil had in mind when she wrote the single word "Nurses" in her journal. Undated, it is the last word in Weil's last journal entry before her death. It is more likely that she had different nurses in mind: not those on the home front, but instead those on the front lines. In 1940, Weil had hatched a plan for the creation of groups of nurse volunteers who would serve alongside soldiers in active battle. Over the course of the next two years, she sought to sell the plan to almost everyone who was someone in political or military circles. In July 1942, just days after arriving in New York with her parents, she wrote to the influential theologian Jacques Maritain, who was also in New York, with a copy of her plan. Her far-fetched hope that Maritain could or would arrange a meeting between her and President Roosevelt never materialized, of course. Weil had no better luck with a letter sent with the same goal to Admiral Leahy, who had served as US ambassador to Vichy until 1942. Increasingly frantic, she then sent a letter to an English officer she had heard on a BBC broadcast, asking him to "read attentively" the copy of the plan she included in the envelope. Her request for his intervention came to naught, as well.[40]

Desperate but not (yet) despondent, Weil also made her pitch in a letter to her friend Maurice Schumann. All that Weil said of the plan, a copy of which she included, was that it "might save the lives of many soldiers, considering the number of deaths in battle due to the lack of immediate care (cases of 'shock,' 'exposure,' loss of blood)." By way of underscoring this claim, Weil attached an extract from the *Bulletin of the American College of Surgeons*, which asserted that the "early application of simple or therapeutic measures can frequently prevent shock or overcome mild shock."[41] But this was largely an afterthought for Weil. Though her "Plan for an Organization of Front-Line Nurses" runs several pages, Weil has next to nothing to say about the usual work of nurses. By the first few pages, the reader realizes that those with more than an "elementary knowledge of nursing" need not apply. The immediate reason was practical. As Weil observed, the nurses would be laboring in combat conditions, under fire just like the soldiers. As a result, they could do little more than apply "dressings, tourniquets, and perhaps injections."[42] In the hope that she would lead the first group of volunteers, Weil herself took a first-aid course in London.

But such activities were fundamentally beside the point. Almost immediately, Weil pivots to the plan's real purpose. The women who volunteered for assignment would do so not to save the lives of wounded soldiers, but instead to offer up their own lives. They were prepared, of course, to bandage wounds. More important, though, they were prepared, even willing, to bleed and die themselves. Weil matter-of-factly notes that these "women would need to have a good deal of courage. They would need to offer their lives as a sacrifice . . . ready to be always at the most dangerous places and to face as much if not more danger than the soldiers who are facing the most."[43]

This idea, Weil allowed, might "appear impractical at first sight because of its novelty." What may seem to be a jab at black humor is nothing of the sort. Weil could not be more serious, for the simple reason that the stakes could not be more serious. She observes, rightly, that German military successes were a matter not just of strategy and material, but also of spirit and men: "Hitler has never lost sight of the essential need to strike everybody's imagination." What better example, she asks, than the Nazi SS (Schutzstaffel). These are men who "are prepared not only for risking their lives but for death. That is the essential point. They have a different inspiration from the rest of the army, an inspiration resembling a faith or a religious spirit." Though we despise what they believe in, Weil warns, we cannot deny the power of those beliefs. The trick was not to copy Nazism's brutal idolatry, Weil noted, but instead to create its opposite. In order to meet this challenge, the Allies needed to mobilize something more than men and material—namely, a moral vitality that, while utterly different from Nazism, is nevertheless its psychological equivalent. "It may be that our victory depends upon the presence among us of a corresponding inspiration, but authentic and pure."[44]

For a Christian, God is the corresponding inspiration; for a Platonist, the Good fits the same bill. Both one and the other are what Murdoch calls "a single, perfect, transcendent, nonrepresentable and necessarily real object of attention."[45] The reality of this object makes itself manifest in our grasp of the world. It does so in the same fashion, Murdoch suggests in a subtle riff on the ontological argument for God's existence, as does the idea of perfection. "A deep understanding of any field of human activity involves an increasing revelation of there being in fact little that is very good and nothing that is perfect. Increasing understanding of human conduct operates in a similar way. We come to perceive scales, distances, standards, and may incline to see as less than excellent what previously we were prepared to 'let by' . . . The idea of perfection works thus within a field of study, producing an increasing sense of direction."[46]

Just as we reveal an orientation toward perfection in our everyday judgments, so too can we orient ourselves toward beauty or goodness. Instances of great goodness—what took place, for example, at Le Chambon-sur-Lignon—pull on our attention, just as instances of great art do, by pulling us away from the unreality of our selfish concerns and toward the reality of the world. Weil would no doubt agree with Murdoch's claim that this entails the truest form of realism. "The authority of the Good seems to us something necessary because the realism (ability to perceive reality) required for goodness is a kind of intellectual ability to perceive what is true, which is automatically at the same time the suppression of self."[47]

In a fundamental sense, Weil's conception of front-line nurses was less a plan than it was a gesture toward beauty and goodness. Having fallen to her knees before images in the fishing village in Portugal and frescoes in Italy, having fallen to her knees in Solesmes while listening to Gregorian chants, it was as if she now fell to her knees before this remarkable tableau she imagined of suffering and sacrifice. It was her way of pointing the viewer away from the always plentiful instances of cynicism, cruelty, and callousness, and toward this imagined act of goodness. "There could be no better symbol of our inspiration than the corps of women suggested here. The mere persistence of a few humane services in the very center of the battle, the climax of inhumanity, would be a signal defiance of the inhumanity which the enemy has chosen for himself and which he compels us also to practice . . . A small group of women exerting day after day a courage of this kind would be a spectacle so new, so significant, and charged with such obvious meaning, that it would strike the imagination more than any of Hitler's conceptions have done."[48]

It would be an understatement to describe the plan—like so much else in Weil's work and life—as impractical. But its impractical character, as with the actions of the villagers of Le Chambon, does not detract from its importance—to the contrary. While living in Marseille and seeking ways to resist, Weil wrote a short essay touching on the Good. Titled "Morale et littérature," the essay contrasted the ease of depicting goodness in art with the difficulty of acting upon it in life. Why is this? While most artists can do as they wish in a novel or painting, Weil replies, they cannot do the same in the world. Unlike the world of art, the world of things obeys gravity. For this reason, Weil asserts, a "man coming down a ladder who misses a rung and falls, presents a sad and uninteresting spectacle." But we would never weary of the sight "of someone walking up to the clouds on air and then downwards, as if he were on a ladder." Without a pause, Weil declares that "it is the same with pure good." Were we to see such an "unfathomable marvel" as we went about our lives, would we not be transfixed, perhaps even transformed, by the sight?

Epilogue

Ideas come and settle in my mind by mistake, then, realizing their mistake, they absolutely insist on coming out. I do not know where they come from, or what they are worth, but, whatever the risk, I do not think I have the right to prevent this operation.

SIMONE WEIL

"The present period is one of those when everything that seems normally to constitute a reason for living dwindles away, when one must, on pain of sinking into confusion or apathy, call everything in question again. The triumph of authoritarian and nationalist movements should blast almost everywhere the hopes that well-meaning people had placed in democracy . . . We are living through a period bereft of a future. Waiting for that which is to come is no longer a matter of hope, but of anguish."[1]

Everything and nothing has changed since Weil made this observation nearly a century ago. In the 1930s, robotization and artificial intelligence were the stuff of Jules Verne or H. G. Wells, yet they were foreseen by Weil's insights into the interlocking nature of capitalism and technology. Though the West withstood the plague of totalitarianism—at least in its Hitlerian and Stalinist guises—in Weil's lifetime, her analysis of these phenomena casts a sharp light on the resurgence of authoritarianism and ethno-nationalism in our own century. Her reflections on the ramifying and relentless nature of force framed the displacement and destruction of entire peoples in her own time, but also the plight of the tens of millions of refugees in our own age.

You might be wondering why, given the persistence of these political and social evils, we should bother to read Weil. After all, many of her answers to these ills were at best impractical and at worst inhuman. In the former case, Weil's argument for the abolition of all political parties—an admittedly attractive option for America in our polarized time—makes sense as a philosophical provocation, but not as practical policy. In the latter case, de Gaulle was not alone to dismiss as crazy Weil's proposal to parachute nurses onto battlefields. I confess I also find it insensate, if not quite insane. Were there not women who, hobbled by the era's many social and institutional prejudices, nevertheless made invaluable contributions? Consider the life of Dr. Louisa Garrett Anderson, an English suffragette who, at the turn of the twentieth century, overcame daunting obstacles to establish hospitals in Paris and London to treat wounded soldiers during World War I. Like Weil, Anderson insisted on the imperative of duty and the conviction that "to do nothing is really too feeble." Like Weil, Anderson insisted on wearing white uniforms (though she and the other female doctors also wore their suffragette pins). Unlike Weil, she and her colleagues did something of vital and lasting importance for others that did not entail martyrdom.[2]

Simone Pétrement makes a poignant confession in her biography of her friend: "Who would not be ashamed of oneself in Simone's presence, seeing the life she led?"[3] This has often been my experience with Weil. Reading her is always a revelation and a reproach. I have never met, and will never meet, the expectations she had of herself and others. But, to be honest, I have also felt at times the irritation and impatience that many who met her also felt, exasperated by her extreme character, confused not just by some of her philosophical ideals, but also by her insistence upon enacting them in our lives. "What I cannot stand," she told her students, "is compromise."[4]

Well, neither can I. But compromise is, almost always, the most I can expect of myself. I know I can never come close to meeting the ideals Weil exacted of herself. In his recent book *A Decent Life: Morality for the Rest of Us*, the philosopher Todd May makes a compelling case for a moral life situated between mediocrity and extremity. "Most of us are incapable of living lives that are beacons of moral light," he sensibly writes, yet we also "desire to be morally decent people." The problem with ideals is that they are, well, ideals. They are, by definition, impossible to live up to for nearly all of us. Besides, as May argues, if we could somehow live up to them, our lives would be less fulfilling and meaningful. The kind of moral life demanded by the categorical imperative (whether or not in skirts), May writes, "requires a great deal of sacrifice and focus, often turning us away from our most important commitments and toward ways of living that, while admirable, are onerous and even impossible for many of us to achieve."[5]

This strikes me as the case with Simone Weil. In a merciless essay, Susan Sontag captured the dilemma faced by many of Weil's readers. Noting the odd, yet powerful attraction of Weil's "sense of acute personal and intellectual extremity," Sontag believed that no more than a "handful of tens of thousands of readers she has won since the posthumous publication of her books and essays really share her ideas."[6] I cannot speak for the tens of thousands of other readers, but I, for one, often find myself in the untenable position of sharing her ideas and yet being aware they cannot be, and perhaps should not be, acted upon. But, like Sontag, I struggle to reconcile Weil's belief in the necessity of mercy with her merciless attitude toward not just foes, but also friends—and of course toward her own self. She deserved far better, as many of her friends did.

But at the same time, I cannot resist returning time and again to this remarkable individual. Weil's life was exemplary, fusing beliefs, words, and acts into a brilliant whole. For many of her readers, Weil's life has all the trappings of secular sainthood. Yet it is wise to recall George Orwell's remarks on a contemporary of Weil's, Mahatma Gandhi. Marveling over the rigor of his spiritual and ethical convictions, which on one occasion led him to accept the death of a family member rather than allow the person to ingest chicken broth, Orwell muses: "This attitude is perhaps a noble one, but, in a sense which—I think—most people would give the word, it is inhuman." His conclusion is clear: "No doubt alcohol, tobacco, and so forth, are things that a saint must avoid, but sainthood is also a thing that human beings must avoid."[7]

But this, of course, does not mean that we can afford to disregard Weil's life any more than Gandhi's life. On the contrary. As with her life, so too with her ideas: they perplex and provoke, dazzle and inspire. More rarely they console, but perhaps consolation is not all that it is cracked up to be. More important, perhaps, is comprehension. "Only the greatest art," Murdoch noted, "invigorates without consoling."[8] This insight applies to Weil's thought and life. One reason she commands our attention is the close correspondence between her thoughts and her actions. At times, this made her insufferable, but it will always make her irreplaceable. What Weil wrote about the salutary stubbornness of reality applies to her thinking and acting: "The source of any kind of virtue lies in the shock produced by the human intelligence being brought up against a matter devoid of lenience and falsity."[9] It is difficult to find a more desirable, if difficult, guide for our own lives.

Acknowledgments

I would not and could not have written this book were it not for Priya Nelson. Not only did Priya first suggest that I write on Simone Weil, but she has since been the very best of editors. I can never thank her enough for the humor and humanity, intelligence and insightfulness she has given since we began this book. I must also thank her editorial assistants, Dylan Montanari and Tristan Bates, for all they have done to help me over the past two years. As for the manuscript's two anonymous readers, I am deeply grateful for their many suggestions and corrections. In addition, I owe a great debt of gratitude to my copyeditor, Lys Weiss of Post Hoc Academic Publishing Services, for her unfailingly sharp eye. My heartfelt thanks, as well, to Christine Schwab and Alan Thomas for their remarkable patience and attentiveness. Finally, I thank Jennifer Johnston for her work on the index. I hope that no one who has played a role in the making of the manuscript will be too disappointed in the book they now have in their hands.

Over the past few years, I have published several articles on Weil that contributed to the writing of this book. I am very grateful to Laura Secor at *Foreign Affairs*, Peter Catapano at the *New York Times*, Fred Hiatt at the *Washington Post*, Paul Jump at *Times Higher Education*, and Boris Dralyuk at the *Los Angeles Review of Books* for all they did, as editors and colleagues, to push me to think more clearly about Weil's thought. For these earlier explorations, see "Rooting for a New Patriotism: Simone Weil Is More Relevant Than Ever, 70 Years On," *Foreign Affairs*,

June 28, 2019; "What We Owe to Others: Simone Weil's Radical Reminder," *New York Times*, February 20, 2018; "This French Intellectual Diagnosed America's Current Political Malaise— in 1943," *Washington Post,* July 18, 2019; "Learning Outcomes Miss the Point of Higher Education," *Times Higher Education*, March 29, 2018; and "The Logic of the Rebel: On Simone Weil and Albert Camus," *Los Angeles Review of Books*, March 7, 2020.

Closer to home, my thanks go to my good friend and colleague Michael Barnes for his close and generous reading of the entire manuscript. Other friends and colleagues to whom I am grateful for reading and commenting on parts of the book are George Alliger and Ronald Collins. As, always, I am very fortunate for the support and friendship offered by William Monroe, dean of the Honors College at the University of Houston, the remarkable place where I have happily worked for the past thirty years.

Finally, I am grateful to my wife, Julie Zaretsky; without her attention, this world and this writer would be infinitely poorer. I am also thankful for all that my stepson, Ruben, has given me over many years. This book is dedicated to my daughter, Louisa, who spends so much of her time thinking.

Notes

INTRODUCTION

1 Francine du Plessix Gray, *Simone Weil* (New York: Viking, 2001), 212.

2 Simone Weil, *First and Last Notebooks*, trans. Richard Rees (Oxford: Oxford University Press, 1970), 335.

3 Weil, *First and Last Notebooks*, 335.

4 Weil, *First and Last Notebooks*, 335.

5 Gray, *Simone Weil*, 26.

6 Costica Bradatan, *Dying for Ideas: The Dangerous Lives of the Philosophers* (London: Bloomsbury, 2015), 7.

7 Simone Pétrement, *La Vie de Simone Weil* (Paris: Fayard, 1973), 21–23.

8 Pétrement, *La Vie de Simone Weil*, 26.

9 Pétrement, *La Vie de Simone Weil*, 45.

10 Gray, *Simone Weil*, 9.

11 Simone Weil, *Waiting for God*, trans. Emma Craufurd (New York: Harper, 2009), 23.

12 Gray, *Simone Weil*, 47.

13 Pétrement, *La Vie de Simone Weil*, 179.

14 Reprinted in *Simone Weil*, ed. Emmanuel Gabellieri and François L'Yvonnet (Paris: Éditions de L'Herne, 2014), 249.

15 Eugen Weber, *The Hollow Years* (New York: W. W. Norton, 1996), 34.

16 Pascal David, "Avec toute l'âme: Simone Weil et la philosophie," in *Simone Weil*, ed. Gabellieri and L'Yvonnet, 94.

17 Pétrement, *La Vie de Simone Weil*, 657.

18 Simone Weil, *Seventy Letters*, trans. Richard Rees (Oxford: Oxford University Press, 1965), 156.

19 Pétrement, *La Vie de Simone Weil*, 667.

20 Pétrement's biography remains the standard account of Weil's life. A professional philosopher, Pétrement was a close friend of Weil. Yet, while her monumental account is sympathetic, it does not, for the most

part, blunt the sharp angles to Weil's character. Unfortunately for those who do not read French, the English translation of Pétrement's book is heavily edited. There are several other biographies in English, many of which veer toward the hagiographic. Francine du Plessix Gray's short and sober account is an admirable exception, despite her insistent diagnosis of Weil as a textbook anorexic.

21 Jenny Odell, *How to Do Nothing: Resisting the Attention Economy* (New York: Melville House, 2019), 101.

22 Matthew Crawford, *Shop Class as Soulcraft* (New York: Penguin, 2009), 16.

23 Iris Murdoch, *Existentialists and Mystics* (New York: Penguin, 1996), 157.

CHAPTER ONE

1 Richard Kuisel, "Auguste Detoeuf, Conscience of French Industry: 1926–1947," *International Review of Social History* 20 (1975): 150.

2 "Factory Journal," in *Simone Weil: Formative Writings, 1929–1941*, ed. Dorothy Tuck McFarland and Wilhelmina Van Ness (Amherst: University of Massachusetts Press, 1987), 155.

3 Anne Reynaud, *Simone Weil: Lectures on Philosophy*, trans. Hugh Price (Cambridge: Cambridge University Press, 1978), 25.

4 Pétrement, *La Vie de Simone Weil*, 148.

5 Simone Weil, *Oppression and Liberty*, trans. Arthur Wills and John Petrie (London: Routledge, 2001), 42.

6 Pétrement, *La Vie de Simone Weil*, 144.

7 Weil, *Oppression and Liberty*, 38.

8 Weil, *Oppression and Liberty*, 53.

9 Weil, *Oppression and Liberty*, 65.

10 Weil, *Oppression and Liberty*, 64.

11 Weil, "Factory Journal," in *Simone Weil: Formative Writings, 1929–1941*, ed. McFarland and Van Ness, 198.

12 Weil, "Factory Journal," in *Simone Weil: Formative Writings, 1929–1941*, ed. McFarland and Van Ness, 160.

13 Weil, "Factory Journal," in *Simone Weil: Formative Writings, 1929–1941*, ed. McFarland and Van Ness, 171.

14 Weil, "Factory Journal," in *Simone Weil: Formative Writings, 1929–1941*, ed. McFarland and Van Ness, 156.

15 Weil, "Factory Journal," in *Simone Weil: Formative Writings, 1929–1941*, ed. McFarland and Van Ness, 203.

16 Weil, "Factory Journal," in *Simone Weil: Formative Writings, 1929–1941*, ed. McFarland and Van Ness, 157.

17 Weil, "Factory Journal," in *Simone Weil: Formative Writings, 1929–1941*, ed. McFarland and Van Ness, 162.

18 Weil, "Factory Journal," in *Simone Weil: Formative Writings, 1929–1941*, ed. McFarland and Van Ness, 159.

19 Weil, "Factory Journal," in *Simone Weil: Formative Writings, 1929–1941*, ed. McFarland and Van Ness, 162.

20 Quoted in Bernard Crick, *George Orwell: A Life* (New York: Little, Brown, 1980), 107.

21 George Orwell, *Down and Out in Paris and London* (New York: Harcourt, Brace, Jovanovich, 1961), 106.

22 Orwell, *Down and Out in Paris and London*, 116.

23 Weil, "The Love of God and Affliction," in *Waiting for God*, 69.

24 Weil, "The Love of God and Affliction," in *Waiting for God*, 69.

25 "The Book of Job," in *The Wisdom Books* (New York: W. W. Norton, 2011), trans. Robert Alter, 21.

26 Weil, *First and Last Notebooks*, 327.

27 Weil, "The Love of God and Affliction," in *Waiting for God*, 72.

28 Weil, "The Love of God and Affliction," in *Waiting for God*, 70.

29 Weil, *Seventy Letters*, 104.

30 Weil, *Seventy Letters*, 104.

31 H. R. Kedward, *France and the French* (New York: Abrams, 2006), 243.

32 Richard Vinen, *The Unfree French* (New Haven, CT: Yale University Press, 2007), 30.

33 Pétrement, *La Vie de Simone Weil*, 515.

34 *Simone Weil*, ed. Gabellieri and L'Yvonnet, 29.

35 *Simone Weil*, ed. Gabellieri and L'Yvonnet, 496.

36 Weil, "The *Iliad*, or the Poem of Force," in *Simone Weil: An Anthology*, ed. Sian Miles (New York: Grove, 2000), 163.

37 Weil, "The *Iliad*, or the Poem of Force," in *Simone Weil: An Anthology*, ed. Miles, 164.

38 Weil, "The *Iliad*, or the Poem of Force," in *Simone Weil: An Anthology*, ed. Miles, 189.

39 Weil, "The *Iliad*, or the Poem of Force," in *Simone Weil: An Anthology*, ed. Miles, 163.

40 Homer, *The Iliad*, trans. Robert Fagles (New York: Viking, 1990), 523.

41 This phrase is taken from the title of the poet Christopher Logue's *All*

Day Permanent Red, one of four books in which he "adapts" the *Iliad* into modern English.

42 Weil, "The *Iliad*, or the Poem of Force," in *Simone Weil: An Anthology*, ed. Miles, 174.

43 Weil, "The *Iliad*, or the Poem of Force," in *Simone Weil: An Anthology*, ed. Miles.

44 Weil, "The *Iliad*, or the Poem of Force," in *Simone Weil: An Anthology*, ed. Miles, 171.

45 Weil, *Oppression and Liberty*, 62.

46 Peter Winch, *Simone Weil: The Just Balance* (Cambridge: Cambridge University Press, 1989), 148.

47 Homer, *The Iliad*, trans. Fagles, 605. In his introduction to Weil's essay, Christopher Benfey identifies these discrepancies. See *War and the Iliad: Simone Weil and Rachel Bespaloff* (New York: NYRB, 2005), xiv–xv.

48 "The Power of Words," in *Simone Weil: An Anthology*, ed. Miles, 225.

49 Simone Weil, "Are We Heading for a Proletarian Revolution," in *Oppression and Liberty*, 5.

50 Weil, *First and Last Notebooks*, 83.

51 Weil, *Selected Essays*, trans. Richard Rees (Eugene, OR: Wipf & Stock, 2015), 36.

52 Winch, *Simone Weil: The Just Balance*, 153.

53 Pétrement, *La Vie de Simone Weil*, 527–28.

54 Weil, *Waiting for God*, 22.

55 Weil, *Waiting for God*, 26.

56 Weil, *Waiting for God*, 26.

57 Weil, "The Love of God and Affliction," in *Waiting for God*, 73.

58 Weil, *Gravity and Grace*, trans. Emma Crawford and Mario von der Ruhr (New York: Routledge, 2002), 28.

59 Weil, *Gravity and Grace*, 26.

60 Weil, *Gravity and Grace*, 4.

61 Weil, *Gravity and Grace*, 377.

62 Weil, *Gravity and Grace*, 327.

63 Mary Dietz, *Between the Human and the Divine: The Political Thought of Simone Weil* (London: Rowman & Littlefield, 1988), 120.

64 Kuisel, "Auguste Detoeuf, Conscience of French Industry: 1926–1947," 151–52.

65 Quoted in Thomas Nevin, *Simone Weil: Portrait of a Self-Exiled Jew* (Chapel Hill: University of North Carolina Press, 1991), 141.

CHAPTER TWO

1   Pétrement, *La Vie de Simone Weil*, 531.
2   *Simone Weil: Late Philosophical Writings*, trans. Eric Springsted and Lawrence Schmidt (Notre Dame, IN: University of Notre Dame Press, 2015), 22 (emphasis added).
3   *Simone Weil: Late Philosophical Writings*, trans. Springsted and Schmidt, 22.
4   *Simone Weil: Late Philosophical Writings*, trans. Springsted and Schmidt, 23.
5   *Simone Weil: Late Philosophical Writings*, trans. Springsted and Schmidt, 25.
6   *Simone Weil: Late Philosophical Writings*, trans. Springsted and Schmidt, 25.
7   *Simone Weil: Late Philosophical Writings*, trans. Springsted and Schmidt, 27.
8   Winch, *Simone Weil: The Just Balance*, 115.
9   Winch, *Simone Weil: The Just Balance*, 118.
10 William James, *Principles of Psychology* (New York: Henry Holt, 1890), 403.
11 Anne Reynaud, *Simone Weil: Leçons de philosophie* (Paris: Gallimard, 1951), 7.
12 Weil, *Waiting for God*, 3.
13 Weil, *Waiting for God*, 61.
14 Weil, *Waiting for God*, 58.
15 Weil, *Waiting for God*, 57.
16 Weil, *Waiting for God*, 58.
17 Weil, *Waiting for God*, 62.
18 Weil, *Waiting for God*, 62–63.
19 Weil, *Waiting for God*, 64.
20 Weil, *First and Last Notebooks*, 327.
21 Simone Weil, *Lectures on Philosophy*, trans. Hugh Price (London: Cambridge University Press, 1978), 95.
22 Weil, *Lectures on Philosophy*, trans. Price, 59.
23 Dietz, *Between the Human and the Divine*, 100.
24 Winch, *Simone Weil: The Just Balance*, 182.
25 See, in particular, Pierre Hadot, *Philosophy as a Way of Life*, ed. Arnold Davidson (New York: Wiley, 1995); and Hadot, *What Is Ancient Philosophy?*, trans. Michael Chase (Cambridge, MA: Belknap, 2004).

26 Introduction to Weil, *First and Last Notebooks*, viii.

27 Simone Weil, *Oeuvres complètes* (Paris: Gallimard, 2006), 6:2, 217. Hereafter cited as *OC*.

28 Weil, *First and Last Notebooks*, 266.

29 *OC*, 6:1, 144.

30 Weil, *First and Last Notebooks*, 4–5.

31 Weil, *First and Last Notebooks*, 19–20.

32 Weil, *First and Last Notebooks*, 31.

33 Weil, *First and Last Notebooks*, 11.

34 Weil, *First and Last Notebooks*, 71.

35 Weil, *First and Last Notebooks*, 97.

36 Winch, *Simone Weil: The Just Balance*, 105–6.

37 The classical philosopher Paul Woodruff explores the meanings of the word in his lovely *Reverence: Renewing a Forgotten Virtue* (Oxford, 2001).

38 Weil, *Waiting for God*, 64–65.

39 *Simone Weil: An Anthology*, ed. Miles, 50.

40 Weil, *Waiting for God*, 72.

41 Iris Murdoch, *The Sovereignty of Good* (London: Routledge, 2007), 55.

42 Weil, *Waiting for God*, 64.

CHAPTER THREE

1 Weil, *Seventy Letters*, 105.

2 Georges Bernanos, *Les Grands cimetières sous la lune* (Paris: Plon, 1938), 169–70.

3 Nevin, *Simone Weil: Portrait of a Self-Exiled Jew*, 104.

4 Pierre Broué and Émile Temime, *The Revolution and the Civil War in Spain* (Cambridge, MA: MIT Press, 1972), 59.

5 According to Weil, Durruti had given one prisoner, a fifteen-year-old fighting with the Franquists, twenty-four hours to renounce Franco and join the anarchists. The boy rejected the offer, and Durruti had him shot (Pétrement, *La Vie de Simone Weil*, 394).

6 Pétrement, *La Vie de Simone Weil*, 389.

7 Pétrement, *La Vie de Simone Weil*, 396.

8 Weil, *Seventy Letters*, 108.

9 *Orwell: Collected Essays, Journalism and Letters*, ed. Sonia Orwell and Ian Angus (New York: Harcourt Brace Jovanovich, 1968), 2:254.

10   Pétrement, *La Vie de Simone Weil*, 395.

11   Simone Weil, *Écrits historiques et politiques* (Paris: Gallimard, 1960), 214.

12   Weil, *Seventy Letters*, 106.

13   George Orwell, *Homage to Catalonia* (New York: Harcourt, 1952), 181.

14   Nevin, *Simone Weil: Portrait of a Self-Exiled Jew*, 16.

15   Alain, *Propos sur les pouvoirs* (Gallimard: Paris, 1993), 61.

16   Pétrement, *La Vie de Simone Weil*, 49.

17   Pétrement, *La Vie de Simone Weil*, 60.

18   Pétrement, *La Vie de Simone Weil*, 71.

19   Pétrement, *La Vie de Simone Weil*, 75.

20   Simone de Beauvoir, *Memoirs of a Dutiful Daughter* (New York: Harper & Row, 1974), 243.

21   Pétrement, *La Vie de Simone Weil*, 103.

22   Jacques Cabaud, *Simone Weil: A Fellowship in Love* (New York: Channel Press, 1964), 38.

23   Pétrement, *La Vie de Simone Weil*, 83.

24   Weil, *La Condition ouvrière* (Paris: Gallimard, 1951), 304.

25   Pétrement, *La Vie de Simone Weil*, 68.

26   Weil, *La Condition ouvrière*, 12.

27   Cabaud, *Simone Weil: A Fellowship in Love*, 58.

28   Cabaud, *Simone Weil: A Fellowship in Love*, 58.

29   Weil, *Oppression and Liberty*, 105.

30   Weil, *Oppression and Liberty*, 102.

31   Hannah Arendt, *Eichmann in Jerusalem: A Report on the Banality of Evil* (New York: Penguin, 1964), 285.

32   Weil, *Oppression and Liberty*, 112.

33   Weil, *Oppression and Liberty*, 42.

34   Weil, *Lectures on Philosophy*, trans. Price, 178.

35   Weil, "Are We Heading for the Proletarian Revolution?," in *Oppression and Liberty*, 22.

36   Weil, "Are We Heading for the Proletarian Revolution?," in *Oppression and Liberty*, 81.

37   Weil, "Are We Heading for the Proletarian Revolution?," in *Oppression and Liberty*, 64.

38   Weil, "Are We Heading for the Proletarian Revolution?," in *Oppression and Liberty*, 79.

39   Weil, "Are We Heading for the Proletarian Revolution?," in *Oppression and Liberty*, 81.

40 Weil, "Are We Heading for the Proletarian Revolution?," in *Oppression and Liberty*, 112.

41 George Orwell, *The Road to Wigan Pier* (New York: Harcourt Brace, 1958), 34.

42 Pétrement, *La Vie de Simone Weil*, 188.

43 Pétrement, *La Vie de Simone Weil*, 188–89.

44 Pétrement, *La Vie de Simone Weil*, 372–73.

45 *The Need for Roots*, trans. Arthur Wills (New York: Routledge, 2002), 250.

46 Gabriella Fiori, *Simone Weil: An Intellectual Biography*, trans. Joseph Berrigan (Athens: University of Georgia Press, 1989), 58.

47 Dietz, *Between the Human and the Divine*, 67.

48 Hannah Arendt, *The Human Condition* (Chicago: University of Chicago Press, 1958), 131.

49 Arendt, *The Human Condition*, 87.

50 Weil, *La Condition ouvrière*, 93.

51 Alain, *Le Premier intellectuel* (Paris: Stock, 2006), 330.

52 Quoted in Fiori, *Simone Weil: An Intellectual Biography*, 44.

53 Pétrement, *La Vie de Simone Weil*, 99–100.

54 Pétrement, *La Vie de Simone Weil*, 206.

55 Fiori, *Simone Weil: An Intellectual Biography*, 143.

56 Nevin, *Simone Weil: Portrait of a Self-Exiled Jew*, 97.

57 Pétrement, *La Vie de Simone Weil*, 467.

58 Weil, *Oppression and Liberty*, 121.

59 Cabaud, *Simone Weil: A Fellowship in Love*, 185–86.

60 Pétrement, *La Vie de Simone Weil*, 487.

61 Pétrement, *La Vie de Simone Weil*, 197.

62 Orwell, "Pacifism and the War," in *Orwell: Collected Essays, Journalism and Letters*, ed. S. Orwell and Angus, 2:226.

63 Weil, *First and Last Notebooks*, 345.

64 Quoted in John Lukacs, "Resistance: Simone Weil," *Salmagundi* 85–86 (Winter–Spring 1990): 115.

65 Sylvie Courtine-Denamy, *Three Women in Dark Times: Edith Stein, Hannah Arendt, Simone Weil* (Ithaca, NY: Cornell University Press, 2000), 158–59.

66 Pétrement, *La Vie de Simone Weil*, 65.

67 Georges Canguilhem, *Vie et mort de Jean Cavaillès* (Paris: Éditions Allia, 1996), 31.

68 Pétrement, *La Vie de Simone Weil*, 668.

69 Quoted in Alan Riding, *And the Show Went On: Cultural Life in Nazi-Occupied Paris* (New York: Alfred A. Knopf, 2010), 219.

70 Fiori, *Simone Weil: An Intellectual Biography*, 37.

71 Sophocles, *Antigone*, trans. Dudley Fitts and Robert Fitzgerald (New York: Harcourt Brace, 1939), lines 52–54.

72 Simone Weil, *Intimations of Christianity among the Ancient Greeks* (New York: Routledge, 2005).

73 *OC*, 2:55.

74 Pierre Rolland, "Simone Weil et la politique," in *Simone Weil: Lectures politiques*, ed. Valérie Gérard (Paris: Éditions Rue d'Ulm, 2011), 76.

75 Rolland, "Simone Weil et la politique," in *Simone Weil: Lectures politiques*, ed. Gérard, 77.

76 Cabaud, *Simone Weil: A Fellowship in Love*.

77 Albert Camus, *The Plague*, trans. Stuart Gilbert (New York: Vintage, 1991), 51.

78 Richard H. Bell, *Simone Weil: The Way of Justice as Compassion* (Oxford: Rowman & Littlefield, 1998), 2.

79 Albert Camus, *The Rebel*, trans. Stuart Gilbert (New York: Vintage, 1975), 285.

80 Camus, *The Rebel*, 16.

81 Camus, *The Rebel*, 128.

82 Simone Weil, "Reflections Concerning the Causes of Liberty and Social Oppression," in *Oppression and Liberty*, 82.

83 *Simone Weil: An Anthology*, ed. Miles, 175.

84 Albert Camus, "On the Future of Tragedy," in *Lyrical and Critical Essays*, trans. Ellen Conroy Kennedy (New York: Vintage, 2012), 310.

CHAPTER FOUR

1 Weil, *Seventy Letters*, 189.

2 Weil, *Seventy Letters*, 190.

3 Weil, *Seventy Letters*, 178.

4 Weil, *Seventy Letters*, 181.

5 Weil, *Seventy Letters*, 180.

6 Weil, *Seventy Letters*, 186.

7 Frederick Brown, *The Embrace of Unreason: France 1914–1940* (New York: Alfred A. Knopf, 2014), 62.

8 In particular, see his detailed and controversial work *La Droite révolutionnaire: Les origines françaises du fascism, 1885–1914* (Paris: Seuil, 1978).

9 David McClellan, *Utopian Pessimist: The Life and Thought of Simone Weil* (New York: Poseidon, 1990), 257–58.

10 Weil, *The Need for Roots*, 49.

11 Weil, *The Need for Roots*, 44.

12 Weil, *The Need for Roots*, 44.

13 Weil, *The Need for Roots*, 45.

14 Weil, *The Need for Roots*, 68.

15 Weil, *The Need for Roots*, 54.

16 Weil, *The Need for Roots*, 79.

17 Perhaps the nostalgia evoked in Housman's poems for Shropshire ("Farewell to barn and stack and tree, / Farewell to Severn shore. / Terence, look your last at me, / For I come home no more") captured Weil's own longing to return to France. (She most probably did not know that Housman only visited Shropshire long after the work's publication and fame.) Or perhaps, more simply, it was death-haunted verse of youthful lives lost. In the British trenches during World War I, Paul Fussell noted, "everyone read Housman." *The Great War and Modern Memory* (Oxford: Oxford University Press, 2013), 177.

18 Weil, *The Need for Roots*, 114.

19 Weil, *Oppression and Liberty*, 55.

20 Roger Scruton, *Conservatism: An Invitation to the Great Tradition* (New York: St. Martin's Press, 2018).

21 *The Iliad*, book 11, lines 155–59.

22 "The *Iliad*, or The Poem of Force," in *Simone Weil: An Anthology*, ed. Miles, 191.

23 *The Odyssey*, trans. Robert Fagles (New York: Penguin, 1996), 462.

24 Christy Wampole, *Rootedness: The Ramification of a Metaphor* (Chicago: University of Chicago Press, 2016), 75.

25 M. I. Finley, *The World of Odysseus* (New York: Penguin, 1979), 57.

26 Weil, *Seventy Letters*, 144.

27 Weil, *Écrits de Londres* (Paris: Gallimard, 1957), 187.

28 Weil, *The Need for Roots*, 160.

29 Alice Conklin, Sarah Fishman, and Robert Zaretsky, *France and Its Empire since 1870* (New York: Cambridge University Press, 2014), 177.

30 Pétrement, *La Vie de Simone Weil*, 120.

31 Nevin, *Simone Weil: Portrait of a Self-Exiled Jew*, 322.

32 Pétrement, *La Vie de Simone Weil*, 466.

33 Simone Weil, "The Colonial Question and the Destiny of the French People," in *Simone Weil on Colonialism*, ed. J. P. Little (London: Rowman & Littlefield, 2003), 110.

34 Weil, "The Colonial Question and the Destiny of the French People," in *Simone Weil on Colonialism*, ed. Little, 110.

35 Weil, "The Colonial Question and the Destiny of the French People," in *Simone Weil on Colonialism*, ed. Little, 115.

36 Weil, "The Colonial Question and the Destiny of the French People," in *Simone Weil on Colonialism*, ed. Little, 115.

37 Weil, *The Need for Roots*, 148.

38 Weil, *The Need for Roots*, 46.

39 https://www.francetvinfo.fr/replay-radio/histoires-d-info/nos-ancetres-les-gaulois-nous-en-rigolions-aime-cesaire_1833407.html.

40 See Alice Conklin's path-blazing work, *A Mission to Civilize: The Republican Idea of Empire in France and West Africa, 1895–1930* (Palo Alto, CA: Stanford University Press, 1997).

41 *Simone Weil on Colonialism: An Ethic of the Other*, ed. J. P. Little (London: Rowman & Littlefield, 2003), 117.

42 Weil, *The Need for Roots*, 103.

43 Weil, *The Need for Roots*, 127.

44 Weil, *The Need for Roots*, 180.

45 Weil, *The Need for Roots*, 130.

46 Weil, *The Need for Roots*, 106.

47 Weil, *The Need for Roots*, 158.

48 Weil, *The Need for Roots*, 158.

49 Weil, *The Need for Roots*, 169.

50 Weil, *The Need for Roots*, 172.

51 Weil, *The Need for Roots*, 174.

52 Ernest Renan, "Qu'est-ce qu'une nation?," in *Nationalism*, ed. John Hutchinson and Anthony Smith (Oxford: Oxford University Press, 1994), 18.

53 Weil, *The Need for Roots*, 99.

54 Weil, *The Need for Roots*, 106.

55 Quoted in Isaiah Berlin, *Three Critics of the Enlightenment: Vico, Hamann and Herder* (Princeton, NJ: Princeton University Press, 2013), 224.

56 Weil, *The Need for Roots*, 160.
57 Weil, *Gravity and Grace*, 65.
58 Weil, *The Need for Roots*, 224.
59 See, for example, Garry Wills, *Inventing America: Jefferson's Declaration of Independence* (New York: Vintage, 2018).
60 Martha Nussbaum, *Creating Capabilities* (Cambridge, MA: Harvard University Press, 2011), 127.
61 Nussbaum, *Creating Capabilities*, 33.
62 Nussbaum, *Creating Capabilities*, 34.
63 Weil, *The Need for Roots*, 70.
64 Weil, *The Need for Roots*, 71.
65 Pétrement, *La Vie de Simone Weil*, 477.
66 Pétrement, *La Vie de Simone Weil*, 229.
67 *Simone Weil: Late Philosophical Writings*, trans. Eric O. Springsted and Lawrence E. Schmidt (Notre Dame, IN: University of Notre Dame Press, 2015), 154.
68 Weil, *The Need for Roots*, 157.
69 Weil, *The Need for Roots*, 43.
70 John Rawls, *A Theory of Justice* (Cambridge, MA: Harvard University Press, 1999), 3.
71 Michael Sandel, *Justice: What's the Right Thing to Do?* (New York: Farrar, Straus & Giroux, 2010), 220.
72 *Simone Weil: An Anthology*, ed. Miles, 63.
73 *Simone Weil: An Anthology*, ed. Miles, 148.
74 *Simone Weil: An Anthology*, ed. Miles, 97.
75 *Simone Weil: An Anthology*, ed. Miles, 137–38.
76 "Rights versus duties: Reclaiming the History and Language of Human Obligations," https://www.abc.net.au/religion/rights-versus-duties-reclaiming-the-history-and-language-of-huma/10095834.

CHAPTER FIVE

1 Weil, *Waiting for God*, 20.
2 Weil, *Waiting for God*, 8.
3 Jean-Marie Perrin and Gustave Thibon, *Simone Weil As We Knew Her*, trans. Emma Craufurd (London: Routledge, 2003), 116.
4 Pétrement, *La Vie de Simone Weil*, 56.
5 Pétrement, *La Vie de Simone Weil*, 68.

6   Simone Weil, *Intimations of Christianity among the Ancient Greeks* (London: Routledge, 1957), 75.

7   *OC*, 1:57.

8   Weil, *Écrits historiques et politiques*, 85.

9   Robert Chenavier, "Completing Platonism through a Consistent Materialism," in *The Christian Platonism of Simone Weil*, ed. E. Jane Doering and Eric O. Springsted (Notre Dame, IN: University of Notre Dame Press, 2004).

10 *OC*, 1:133.

11 Weil, *Intimations of Christianity*, 77.

12 Yosef Yerushalmi, *Zakhor: Jewish History and Jewish Memory* (New York: Schocken, 1989), 59–60.

13 Gershom Scholem, *Major Trends in Jewish Mysticism* (New York: Schocken, 1961), 261.

14 Weil, *First and Last Notebooks*, 423.

15 Nevin, *Simone Weil: Portrait of a Self-Exiled Jew*, 287.

16 Weil, *Gravity and Grace*, 33.

17 Except when they didn't. In his landmark work *Montaillou*, the historian Emmanuel Leroy Ladurie relates the life of one of the *perfecti* who had a heartwarming weakness for the all-too-physical world of food and women.

18 Weil, *Seventy Letters*, 130.

19 Weil, *Seventy Letters*, 93.

20 Nevin, *Simone Weil: Portrait of a Self-Exiled Jew*, 184.

21 Peter Conradi, *Iris Murdoch: A Life* (New York: W. W. Norton, 2001), 501.

22 Murdoch, *Existentialists and Mystics*, xxvii.

23 Murdoch, *Existentialists and Mystics*, 375.

24 Murdoch, *Existentialists and Mystics*, 51.

25 Murdoch, *Existentialists and Mystics*, 460.

26 Murdoch, *The Sovereignty of Good*, 96–97.

27 Murdoch, *The Sovereignty of Good*, 53.

28 Murdoch, *The Sovereignty of Good*, 376–77.

29 Camus, *The Plague*, 40.

30 Murdoch, *The Sovereignty of Good*, 35–36.

31 Weil, *Intimations of Christianity*, 134.

32 Murdoch, *The Sovereignty of Good*, 90.

33 Murdoch, *The Sovereignty of Good*, 57.

34 Simone Weil, *On the Abolition of All Political Parties*, trans. Simon Leys (Black Inc Books, 2013), 17.

35 Weil, *On the Abolition of All Political Parties*, 5.

36 Weil, *On the Abolition of All Political Parties*, 18.

37 Weil, *On the Abolition of All Political Parties*, 27.

38 Weil, *On the Abolition of All Political Parties*, 16.

39 Pétrement, *La Vie de Simone Weil*, 686.

40 Pétrement, *La Vie de Simone Weil*, 627–28.

41 Weil, *Seventy Letters*, 153.

42 Weil, *Seventy Letters*, 146.

43 Weil, *Seventy Letters*, 146–47.

44 Weil, *Seventy Letters*, 150.

45 Murdoch, *The Sovereignty of Good*, 54.

46 Murdoch, *The Sovereignty of Good*, 60.

47 Murdoch, *The Sovereignty of Good*, 64.

48 Murdoch, *The Sovereignty of Good*, 150–51.

EPILOGUE

1 "Reflections Concerning the Causes of Liberty and Social Oppression," in *Oppression and Liberty*, trans. Arthur Wills and John Petrie (New York: Routledge, 2001), 36–37.

2 See Wendy Moore, *No Man's Land* (New York: Basic Books, 2020), a bracing account of Anderson and what came to be known as the Suffragettes' Hospital.

3 Pétrement, *La Vie de Simone Weil*, 532.

4 Gray, *Simone Weil*, 26.

5 Todd May, *A Decent Life: Morality for the Rest of Us* (Chicago: University of Chicago Press, 2020), 11.

6 Susan Sontag, *Against Interpretation and Other Essays* (New York: Farrar, Straus & Giroux, 1966), 50.

7 George Orwell, "Reflections on Gandhi," in *The Orwell Reader*, ed. Richard Rovere (Harcourt, Brace, Jovanovich, 1956), 332.

8 Iris Murdoch, "Against Dryness," *Encounter* 16 (January 1961).

9 Weil, "Reflections Concerning the Causes of Liberty and Social Oppression," 82.

Index